THE ULTIMATE GUIDE TO
CHOPPERS

THE ULTIMATE GUIDE TO
CHOPPERS

JOHN CARROLL & GARRY STUART

CHARTWELL
BOOKS, INC.

This edition published in 2007 by
CHARTWELL BOOKS, INC.
A division of BOOK SALES, INC.
114 Northfield Avenue
Edison, New Jersey 08837
USA

Copyright © 2007
Regency House Publishing Ltd.

For all editorial enquiries please contact
Regency House Publishing Ltd at

www.regencyhousepublishing.com

ISBN 13: 978-0-7858-2249-3
ISBN 10: 0-7858-2249-6

Printed in China
by Sino Publishing House Ltd.

CONTENTS

INTRODUCTION:
KNEES IN THE BREEZE

Visit any of the truckstops and bars in the towns alongside interstate highways 35 and 40 and the voice of Merle Haggard can be heard drifting from a thousand jukeboxes, 'We don't smoke marijuana in Muskogee, we don't take our trips on LSD, we don't burn our draft cards down on Main Street, 'cos we like living right and being free.' Proud to be an Okie from Muskogee, he continues, 'We don't let our hair grow long and shaggy like the hippies out in San Francisco do ...'

It comes as no surprise, therefore, that Sonny Barger, a longstanding member of the most notorious motorcycle club in the world, failed to find a welcome in Oklahoma. 'We were on the road, tearing through the Texas panhandle and on into Oklahoma. As we approached Oklahoma City, ten or twelve Oklahoma state troopers pulled onto the freeway and escorted us right through the city limits. They didn't even want us stopping for gas.'

Bikers do not like being called hippies, the blue-collar backgrounds of many of them having precluded them from publicly burning their draft cards during the Vietnam War. However, they are happy to take influences

from the counter-culture to their hearts. What would not have been evident to bemused bystanders in Texola, Clinton or El Reno, witnesses to Barger and his brothers thundering east, clinging to the apehangers of their Harleys, was that the outlaw biker movement has its roots in Oklahoma's dust and that these prodigal sons are most definitely the spiritual descendants of those who once travelled west on the same roads, including the famous Route 66.

Makes me no difference wherever I ramble
Lord, wherever I go,
I don't wanna be pushed around by th' police
in yo' town,
I got them 66 Highway Blues.

The 1930s saw a time of widespread westward migration, when the dispossessed and destitute of Oklahoma followed the hillbilly highway to California in search of better lives. It was the Oklahoma of Woody Guthrie songs and John Steinbeck novels, in which '...the people are in flight, and they come into 66 from the tributary side roads, from the wagon tracks and the rutted country roads. 66 is the mother road, the road of flight'.

The first and most affected victims of the Great Depression were those who farmed the arid western prairies. The unemployed of the cities may have regarded the decade as 'the hungry thirties', but it was 'the dirty thirties' to these farmers. Driven from their homes by dust storms, plagues of grasshoppers and the mortgage companies, they loaded their few possessions into broken-down jalopies and took to the road 'looking for a job at honest pay'.

OPPOSITE
Two choppers riding the highway.

LEFT
Harley-Davidsons at Daytona Beach,
Florida.

It's a case of seeing and being seen at Daytona, Sturgis, Laconia, Laughlin and the rest of the big biker gatherings.

The tragic Joad family of Steinbeck's *Grapes of Wrath* is an example of America's dispossessed. It is said that when directing the film of the book, John Ford needed background music for a group scene. He asked the Oklahomans, whom he had recruited as extras, to sing something that was known to every Okie, Arkie and Mizoo. They spontaneously broke into *Goin' Down the Road Feelin' Bad*. This old blues song had long been a favourite of American vagrants and hoboes, but it now assumed a new significance because it described the plight of the refugee so well, more than a million having made the trek west from Oklahoma and the neighbouring states to California.

I'm a-blowin' down this old dusty road,
I'm a-blowin' down this old dusty road,
I'm a-blowin' down this old dusty road, Lord, Lord,
An' I ain't a-gonna be treated this a-way.

In his seminal book on the Hell's Angels of the 1960s, Hunter Thompson recounts that for many of the later arrivals in California it was 'just another hard dollar', but that the coming of the Second World War enabled migrants to find work in a suddenly booming labour market. He wrote: 'It is easy enough to trace the Hell's Angels' mystique – and even their name and emblems – back to the Second World War and Hollywood. But their genes and real history go back a lot farther. The Second World War was not the original California boom but the rebirth of a thing that began in the thirties and was already tapering off when the war economy made California a new Valhalla.'

Referring to a work by Nelson Algren entitled *A Walk on the Wild Side*, Thompson remarks how Algren's migrant 'Linkhorns', for whom drifting had become a habit, eventually wandered into California and into well-paid war-economy jobs. His white trash were Californians, by the time the war ended, which was the result of either time spent in the services or labouring in the cities. 'When the war ended, California was full of veterans looking for ways to spend their separation bonuses. Many decided to stay on the coast,

8

The Boot Hill Saloon is one of the famous watering holes in Daytona Beach, situated across the street from the cemetery.

and while their new radios played hillbilly music they went out and bought big motorcycles – not knowing exactly why, but in the booming, rootless atmosphere of the times, it seemed the thing to do.' From here it was but a short step from white trash to scooter trash. Brock Yates writes in *Outlaw Machine* that it was, '... the hard riding, grease stained independent rabble who would, in a subtly perverse way, ultimately define the image of America's greatest motorcycle'.

The first chapter of the Hell's Angels was formed in 1948 in Berdoo – San Bernardino – California, and Ralph Hubert 'Sonny' Barger, an actual descendant of the original migrant workforce, became a founder member of the Oakland chapter soon afterwards. Other clubs were eventually formed and while Barger's club may have ridden east through Oklahoma, it is two of the other major One Percenter clubs that have charters in Oklahoma City: the Bandidos and the Outlaws.

RIGHT
From left to right: Snob (Hell's Angels Motorcycle Club, London, England), John Carroll (co-author of this book) and Sonny Barger (Hell's Angels MC, Cave Creek, Arizona) at the London book-signing of Sonny Barger's book.

OPPOSITE
A chopped Harley silhouetted against the sky.

The Bandidos MC was formed in Texas during 1966 and although its strongest presence is in the southern states of America, it has chapters worldwide. The Oklahoma City chapter of the Outlaws MC is the westernmost part of an organization that can trace its roots back to thirties Chicago and currently stretches from Detroit and Chicago to Australia and Europe; whether or not the members of these clubs are hard-core bikers or full-time criminals depends on whose opinion is to be believed. Yves Lavigne paints a particularly grim picture in his sensationalist books, while others view the bikers more generously. In his novel of 1991, *Against the Wind*, J.F. Freedman attempts to explain what makes them tick: '... straight society can't handle the truth they lay on the world so they've got to cut them down, categorize them, call them outlaws. Anyway so what if they are outlaws, that's the American way.'

Oklahoma, of course, has its own outlaw tradition in the shape of Pretty Boy Floyd. Floyd was a bank robber during the thirties, immortalized in song by Woody Guthrie, and met his death at the hands of law enforcement officials.

There were other populist outlaws of the same period, including Bonnie and Clyde and John Dillinger. Guthrie was thinking of such outlaws, and particularly of Charles 'Pretty Boy' Floyd and Jesse James, when he remarked, 'No wonder folks likes to hear songs about the Outlaws – they're wrong all right, but not half as dirty and sneakin' as some of our so-called "higher-ups" ...' So it is with outlaw bikers: it is a

theme that has echoed down the years, with references to bikers scattered through both rock and country songs, vignettes of a life on the road. Billy Joe Shaver's *Highway of Life* is typical:
*Oh the outlaws they ride on their two-
wheeled monsters
Like a big giant serpent they glide through
the night
Just shakin' their chains like a diamond
back rattler ...*

Brock Yates, writing in 2000 of the Depression, remarked that 'From this raw underside of life the motorcycle emerged as a "real man's" machine ...'. If the motorcycle is a man's machine – and there are many scooter chicks who'd argue this point – then the chopper is a man's man's machine, though in reality it's probably just a step or two further towards the extreme. Choppers – a blend of form and function – are about motion: going from place to place, whether crossing country or riding from bar to bar. In this they are following the tradition of movement within American society that was documented by Steinbeck, Kerouac and others.

As we have seen, therefore, it has been suggested more than once that some of the original bikers and One Percenters sprang from Okie stock. Indeed, H.R. Kaye's semi-biographical work recounts how the parents of the book's major character, Bill Henderson, arrive in Oakland in exactly this situation, this being one of a series of such migrations; in fact, settlers in North America had been moving west almost since the continent was first discovered. There

had been the gold rush migrations and the long cattle drives, and later there were those who travelled from coast to coast aboard the box cars. Nowadays, it is the long-distance drivers with their 18-wheelers and, of course, the bikers, to whom extreme mobility is part and parcel of their existence.

The lifestyle of the biker fits the American tradition of mobility comfortably, the idea of roaming far and wide having been established early on in the relatively short history of motorcycling. In its earliest days the race was continually on to break transcontinental records and by the outbreak of the Second World War the concept of the Gypsy Tour, sanctioned by the American Motorcyclist Association (AMA) was well established. Nowadays the biker's vernacular is full of terms and phrases that obliquely refer to that mobility, such as sled-bumming, saddle tramp, cycle Gypsy, scooter trash, iron horse, nomad clubs, being in the wind and more. Some of this terminology is clearly borrowed from the Old West and the blues but the meanings are clear. It's all about tyres humming on asphalt. And hum they most certainly do, especially twice a year when the largest gatherings of bikers on the planet make their presence felt.

In early spring there is the Daytona and the chance of some Florida sunshine, guaranteed to dispel the winter blues that still hold the north firmly in their grasp. Then there's Sturgis in late summer, before the fall signals the arrival of winter in lands sacred to Native Americans, and nearby Deadwood, famous as the haunt of old-time outlaws, with Laconia, Laughlin, Biketoberfest and countless smaller events following in their wake.

Daytona and Sturgis are places of pilgrimage where the biking confraternity is concerned. Some attend one or both every year, some only make it once or twice in a lifetime, almost like the hajj to Mecca, but there is a special atmosphere when they do occur, with plenty of drinking and partying, riding and racing, and the making and

renewal of old friendships. Both of these events have developed and changed with the passing of the decades: no longer is there racing on the beach in Daytona, neither is the main street in Deadwood knee-deep in beer cans these days. Moreover, the partying in Sturgis' city park isn't the spectacle it once was since camping was banned, even though the T-shirts still read, 'To hell with the races, I came to party'.

Numerous new bars have opened to cater for the growing number of attendees, with bikers maybe a little more welcome than they once were and tolerated for the money they spend, while some of the yuppie women look good in chaps and the police are on the whole more mellow than in the past. With the certainty that day follows night, there will be Harleys and choppers running up and down Florida's Atlantic coast come March and in August they'll be negotiating the twists and turns of the Black Hills Rally. There is Laconia in New Hampshire, Red River in New Mexico, the Four Corners run to where the boundaries of four states meet, the Laughlin Run in Nevada and others. With the exception of Laconia, these haven't been established as long, but who would ever have imagined the annual events at Daytona and Sturgis enduring for a half-century or more?

At times, attempts have been made to put a stop to these big events. In 1981, the Laconia Classic was in jeopardy when House Bill 635 was introduced by representative Marshall French of Belknap, New Hampshire. The bill was widely acknowledged as an attempt to discourage promoters from scheduling any future

motorcycle events at Loudon in New Hampshire. Then the cover of the June 1981 issue of *Street Chopper* magazine announced 'Daytona '81 – will there be an '82?', after a week of zealous policing, while the T-shirts of the embittered read 'I paid my dues, Daytona Cop Week'. Meanwhile, Daytona Beach's anti-topless dancing edict went into effect one midnight in December 1981 after a circuit judge refused to postpone its implementation.

Time magazine had already given some indication of the prevailing attitudes in 1971 when it posed the question: 'Has any means of transportation ever suffered a worse drubbing than the motorcycle? In the seventeen years since Stanley Kramer put Marlon Brando astride a Triumph in *The Wild One* (1953), big bikes and those who ride them have been made into apocalyptic images of aggression and revolt – Greasy Rider on an iron horse with 74 cubic inch lungs and apehanger bars, booming down the freeway to rape John Doe's daughter behind the white clapboard bank: swastikas, burnt rubber, crab lice and filthy denim ... As an object to provide linked reactions of desire and outrage, the motorcycle has few equals – provided it is big enough ... Anti-social? indeed Yes.'

A decade later, P.J. O'Rourke, writing in *Car and Driver* magazine, summed up the appeal of it all in his inimitable style: 'There is a way that women, women of all ages look at you when you ride a big H-D. It combines disgust and fascination – as though you were walking around in public with your principal organ of reproduction hanging out of your

PAGE 14
Rudi, from California Choppers, astride his chopped FXR.

PAGE 15
Two of the earliest chapters of the Hell's Angels to be established in Europe were in England and Switzerland.

OPPOSITE
The action at Daytona Beach during Bikeweek and Biketoberfest goes on late into the night.

LEFT
Bjorn, a British Hell's Angel, on his rigid-framed Evolution.

pants, but also as though that organ were an exceedingly large one.' As an old biker saying goes, 'When we do right no one remembers, when we do wrong no one forgets'.

Black biker T-shirts frequently feature slogans that reflect the prevailing collective thought of the times, political in some cases, lewd and lascivious in many and frequently cynical – but all are designed to raise a smile. A selection from the early eighties includes:

My ol' lady yes, my dog maybe, my Harley-Davidson NEVER
Screw imports, buy American
Ride hard, die free
The Surgeon General has determined that messing with a Harley rider is dangerous to your health
Rather a sister in a whorehouse than a brother on a Honda
Free Sonny Barger
Harleys don't leak oil, they mark their spot
Don't waste gas, waste Khomeni
Harley riders' ol' ladies do everything better and look better doin' it

A member of the Vietnam Veterans club.

Ride a bike. Go to prison
*It's hard to soar with eagles when you ride
with turkeys*
Chrome don't get you home

A decade or so later things had changed,
but only slightly:

*Pardon me, but I'm a Harley rider and you've
obviously mistaken me for someone who gives
a shit*
Ride American, speak English and be proud
The older I get the better I was
I'd rather have herpes than a Honda
*You never truly know a woman 'til you meet
her in court*
*Sturgis, South Dakota – Home of Police
Harassment 1993*
*Flathead, Knucklehead, Panhead, Shovelhead,
Blockhead, Gimmehead*
You ain't having fun until they dial 911
Life ain't easy when you're fat and greasy
Live to ride, ride to live
Work to ride, ride to work
Put your ass on some class
Ageing is inevitable, maturing is optional
Loud wives lose lives

As the 21st century began to roll, T-shirts
began to read:

Choppers 'til you die
Wanna ride?
*Honk if you've never seen a gun fired from a
moving chopper*
It's a shame that stupidity isn't painful
My lawyer can kick your lawyer's ass
Some people are alive only because it's

illegal to kill them
I spent most of my money on bikes, booze and
broads. I wasted the rest
I rode mine to trailer week
Bikers against Saddam Hussein
Choppers rule
Keep it rigid
Harley Hyphen Davidson
Let those who ride decide
Harley-Davidson. If I had to explain you
wouldn't understand
The old lady said it was her or Sturgis …
Bikers are a rare breed, Harley riders are a
dime a dozen

There are plenty more, possibly too raunchy to quote here. One thing is for certain: it's been a wild roller coaster of a ride down the years and looks like continuing for a long time.

This book is no dry-as-dust, model-by-model history of the Milwaukee marque. It documents a slice of Harley-Davidson action that the factory would rather not have existed. But if there had been no One Percenters and none of the notoriety that ensued, it is likely that the fad for Harley ownership of recent years would not have been so insistent. Nowadays, the factory builds bikes and sells clothing clearly inspired by the biker sub-culture, with the effect that the ordinary man in the street can buy into Harley's watered-down interpretation of the outlaw biker lifestyle merely by stepping across the dealer's threshold. Chopping a Harley involves a much greater degree of commitment to the bike in question and there's much more at stake than its resale value.

Anyone serious about riding a chopper will overcome any number of obstacles in order to do so. It's a long way from a couple of crates of swap-meet parts or a worn-out stocker to splitting lanes on a finished chopper, but the hope is that by reading this book you will know exactly how far that is. The old-style rigid-with-flames chopper pictured here is my own bike. It is a built-from-scratch, rigid flathead that grew out of an olive-drab WLC (Canadian Army 45) engine and transmission. New wheel rims were laced to swap-meet hubs, while yokes were made from billet alloy for the secondhand telescopic forks. A custom rear fender was shortened to suit the lines of the

John Carroll's chopped 45. It comprises a custom-made rigid frame, telescopic front end, apehangers and a Sportster tank. The bike was completed by Phil Piper of Phil's Chopper Shack.

were made to measure, the seat being a one-off. All this and a lot of help from good friends, and the machine was ready to paint.

Having accomplished all of this, there was the hassle of getting a licence plate, but in the end every cent spent, every drop of sweat spilt and all the worry involved is worthwhile. My flathead may not have the biggest engine, nor have had the optimum amount of money spent on it and it definitely isn't the fanciest bike in this book, but it is uniquely mine: rigid frame, Sportster tank way up high, apehanger bars, solo seat, jockey shift, suicide clutch and flame paint. Its lines are intended to be classic, albeit with a few modern touches, and while the same style of bike would have

looked cool with a Panhead motor, here in Europe there's a lot of respect for the 45-cubic inch (737-cc) flathead. They aren't called 'Liberators' for nothing: the Harley is often described as the 'Freedom Machine' and in the case of the 45 flathead this really strikes a chord.

A generation of Americans and Canadians rode them during the Second World War to keep Europe free and it is entirely appropriate that the engines should provide the power for the freedom machines of another generation. Fashions may have changed since it was built, but even as I was selecting the pictures to illustrate this book, it was still the old rigids with springer forks and flame paint jobs that caught my

THIS PAGE and OPPOSITE
The American Bandidos has chapters around the world. Another major American club with numerous chapters is the Sons of Silence, while the Boozefighters is one of the earliest of the One Percenter clubs.

frame that had been made to measure and to accept the diverse selection of components, including an early Evo Sportster gas tank. The handlebars, brake master cylinder, grips, headlight, tail light and numerous small parts were bought over the counter at custom shops, while the forward controls

attention. I'm old-school chopper through and through, but there's room for every type of chopper and scope for everyone's imagination.

I am aware that my motivation to have my own chopper, built from the ground up, is no different from that of many others. For me it was the culmination of a dream, one I had had since the time I first stumbled across *Street Chopper* magazine in a store and discovered Hunter Thompson's book about the Hell's Angels years ago while still at school.

Keith Ball, long-time editor of *Easyriders*, was similarly affected. 'As a young man I dreamed colourful fantasies of flying down endless highways on a custom motorcycle. Gazing at bike magazines was my only outlet into a world separate from my middle-class American life. Until I was sixteen I only stumbled onto three fleeting glimpses of truly custom Harley-Davidsons. I wasn't aware of the sheer power I would someday hold in my sunburnt arms, of the sensual sensation of unleashed freedom, the deep feeling of mechanical accomplishment or the violent world of the outlaw. It was only a wishful dream at the time.'

There is another side that makes this different from other Harley books in that it is chronicling the development of something altogether imprecise. With the exception of certain landmark events – Hollister, the first screening of the *Easy Rider* movie – the casual chopper movement has always been careless of dates. Styles evolved out of others, certain components became passé gradually rather than overnight, people came

ABOVE
Sonny Barger was one of the founders of the Oakland, California, chapter of the Hell's Angels.

RIGHT
Dick Tree riding his rigid-framed big-twin chopper on the highway.

onto the scene while others drifted away, and little was written down, particularly regarding the earliest days. Choppers were often rebuilt and built again and each decade belongs to a different generation of riders.

Magazines and the catalogues of custom parts manufacturers are the only genuine archive material, the exception being a handful of movies. The bikes in *The Wild One*, *Hell's Angels on Wheels*, *Easy Rider* and *Mask* vary widely and are typical of their respective eras. This book presents a primarily American perspective on choppers, simply because that is where they originated, but it is worth noting that the chopper phenomenon really got started in the early seventies in Europe, initially imitating American styles and using many imported parts. Gradually styles unique to Europe developed, the Swedes in particular being noted for building extreme long-forked choppers, while the British continue to build classy choppers with almost any type of

California-based Arlen Ness is one of the world's most famous builders of custom bikes.

The late Karl Smith, also known as Big Daddy Rat, is the founder of the famous Rat's Hole Show at Daytona Beach.

The Pagans MC is a long-established American motorcycle club.

motorcycle engine. There has recently been a fad for 'streetfighters' – racetrack-inspired Harleys with performance sports-bike front ends and monoshock suspension set-ups. Now the chopper has a presence it would have been impossible to imagine even ten years ago.

Ask most people what a chopper is and it is likely they will say 'a motorcycle with long forks'. Press them further and they'll describe it as ridden by 'long-haired biker types'. There are few road users who at one time or another haven't had their senses assaulted by the sight of a chopper riding club, loud and proud, jamming it on, kings of all they survey. Ordinary citizens, mouths agape, are at once fascinated and repelled – what can it be like to ride one of those things? There's a pleasant irony in all this because if one were to ask a motorcyclist, rather than a biker ('bikers being a rare breed, Harley riders are a dime a dozen') what a chopper is, he may well describe it as noisy, dangerous, thrown together and an affront to respectable motorcycling, with other negative images thrown in for good measure. Certainly he will tell you what a sports bike, a trail bike, a roadster, a race replica, a tourer or a moped is, but the truth is that to the non-motorcycling public these are one and the same thing while choppers are different.

Choppers are choppers and are difficult to pinpoint in that there are no large factories with teams of engineers working on their design, as is the case with every other type of motorcycle without exception. There are no lovingly produced brochures listing the

selling points and desirable features. There are no sheets or books filled with the specifications and minutiae of the machine's components and there are no advertising campaigns, yet the chopper is the most recognizable type of motorcycle in the world. 'That ain't no motorcycle, Baby, that's a chopper'. Sadly for the purists, some of this is changing as numerous shops, struggling to satisfy the booming demand for the latest high-tech-style choppers, crank them out in increasing numbers.

The chopper's origins are distant and somewhat vague, the style having evolved from other motorcycles, aided by a few acid-induced dreams and marijuana-inspired delusions. While it is hard to pinpoint its conception, acceptance of the chopper's bona fides can be found in unorthodox places, Angels referring to standard 74s as 'garbage wagons', while Bylaw Number 11 of the charter is a put-down in the grand manner: 'An Angel cannot wear the colors while riding on a garbage wagon with a non-Angel'. This, quoted from Hunter S. Thompson in 1966, illustrates how the chopper as a distinct type of motorcycle became more than simply acknowledged but mandatory within that club.

In the vernacular of that time, a garbage wagon was a stock Harley-Davidson, still equipped with windshield and panniers, a 74 was a Harley-Davidson with 74-ci (1200-cc) displacement: in other words, only choppers were acceptable for club members to ride and their decidedly unofficial, almost underground, origins as the transport of the Hell's Angels and the numerous other clubs

of the era, including Satan's Slaves, Gypsy Jokers, Satan's Sinners and the Jokers out of Hell, among others, ensured that motorcycles and motorcycling would never be the same again. It also meant that choppers began to feature on the front pages of newspapers across the Western world, from whence it was but a short step to movies. The biker on a chopper, rather like the cowboy on his horse, became both hero and anti-hero, subject to the whim of the script writer.

The marked similarity between the old-time outlaws, such as Jesse James and Billy the Kid, hadn't been lost on the new generation of saddle tramps either and it isn't implausible to suggest that both groups had similar origins, coming from similar socio-economic backgrounds and divided only by time. Then, much of everything was new, especially the vehicles, the innovations and maybe the dreams. While some regard chopper riders as the last cowboys, others see them as the last pirates, swashbucklers crossing the globe on Harleys. It is surely no accident that many clubs feature versions of the 'Jolly Roger' on their colours and that many male bikers had their left ears pierced pirate-style long before it was fashionable. Pirates, cowboys, gypsies, tramps or thieves, the enigma on wheels rolls on. It's a never-ending journey, as new as tomorrow and as old as time, tempered by action, danger and the elements, a journey in search of freedom and romance. A long neck and a dollar for the jukebox, 'ladies love outlaws [and hot looking choppers]'... ain't it the truth?

CHAPTER ONE
THE FORTIES & FIFTIES: ORIGINS AND INFLUENCES

The origins of the chopper are inextricably linked with the period of American motorcycling history that spanned the Second World War. As the country emerged from the depths of the Depression, motorcycling became a popular pastime again and the establishment of Class C rules gave it a wider appeal in that 'ordinary' riders were able to compete without the need for specialist race bikes. Class C and the staging of a number of AMA-sanctioned 100- and 200-mile National races in places like Savannah, Georgia, and Daytona, Florida, began to attract huge crowds of spectators.

Many riders adopted the style of the mildly modified race bike for street use, Class C rules stipulating that race bikes be street-legal prior to the race, so that what can be termed pre-war-customs were usually bikes modified with a cut-down or removed front fender and 'bobtailed' (later shortened to 'bobbed') rear fender. Sometimes a front fender was fitted to the back so that the flared end extended much further around the wheel than normal and a pillion pad was put on that, the whole being supported by a modified or specifically fabricated fender

modifications, including redesigned tail lights and tank-mounted dashes. (Both styles of lights and dashes would later appear on custom bikes.)

Meanwhile the war had left its mark on motorcycling in strange ways, leading to the superstition that green Harleys were unlucky. Dispatch riders had been a target for enemy fire because they were carriers of important information. They also had to contend with land mines and wires strung across the road designed to decapitate in forward areas. It was also inevitable, Japan having become a later member of the Axis, that the new-fangled Japanese-manufactured bikes should

OPPOSITE
Paul Bairstow's forties-style bobber. Its styling is based on the bikes eligible for the AMA's Class C racing of the thirties and forties and included cut-down fenders and a pillion pad.

LEFT
Bairstow astride his bobber on Chelsea Bridge in London, England.

BELOW
Huggy Leaver riding his similarly styled big twin, a 1946 UL flathead.

strut. These modifications were made to both Harley-Davidson and Indian motorcycles, reflecting the fact that both were popular American bikes and that much of the race-track rivalry was between the motorcycles of these two companies.

However, motorcycling in general and racing in particular were to be curtailed in the U.S.A. by the outbreak of the Second World War and the Japanese air-strike on Pearl Harbor in Hawaii. An important pre-war development had been the 1936 launch of the overhead-valve EL model of 61-ci (1000-cc) displacement. This was a fast road

bike and although its production span was also interrupted by war it was to have a major effect on motorcycling. Its introduction was one of the factors that gave Harley-Davidson a significant advantage over its last domestic competitor, Indian, of Springfield, Massachusetts.

After the war, servicemen began to return home and many of them were looking for ways to spend the pay that had accumulated to them and to let off steam after years spent in uniform. Harley-Davidson resumed production of the overhead-valve EL models, albeit with a few

ABOVE
Lee, from the British HD45 club, on his bobber at the Old Timers Rally in Holland.

OPPOSITE
Crockers were hand-made in small numbers by a former Indian dealer, Albert Crocker, and can be regarded as the first factory custom motorcycles. Note the hot-rod scalloped paint job on the tank.

be derided as 'Jap crap' and spawn T-shirts and bumper stickers with slogans that read, 'Honda, Kawasaki, Suzuki, Yamaha from the people who brought you Pearl Harbor'.

'Wino' Willie Forkner, a former gunner and engineer in the 7th Air Force and later a charter member of the Boozefighters, one of the earliest One Percenter clubs, summed this up in a 1986 interview in *Easyriders* magazine: 'Yeah, well those damned

riceheads. Son of a bitch I don't understand how, if we won that damned war, it don't look like it. That's the bitch of it – they got the whole country here. It's amazing, I still can't believe it but I guess that's what politics is all about.'

Of the survivors, like Wino Willie, who came back home and and back to their motorcycles, it was back to normal and back to AMA-sanctioned events. For others it

wasn't so straightforward: motorcycle club uniforms and rally games failed to have the same appeal to hardened veterans who had buried their comrades in Europe and on islands in the Pacific.

The author of *From Here to Eternity*, James Jones, sums it up thus: 'About the last thing to go was the sense of esprit. That was the hardest thing to let go of, because there was nothing in civilian life that could replace it – the love and understanding of men for men in dangerous times and places and situations. Just as there was nothing in civilian life that could replace the heavy, turgid day-to-day excitement of danger. Families and other civilian types would never understand that sense of esprit any more than they would understand the excitement of the danger.'

Some found what they were looking for in the saddle of a big motorcycle in the company of buddies who were equally restless and the lure of endless blacktop, accepting that, for better or worse, the world had irrevocably changed. Ed Maye, a Colorado resident, was discharged from the U.S. Navy in 1946 and bought a 74-ci Knucklehead. In 1996, watching Harleys leaving Severance, Colorado, he recalled the back cylinder fouling the plug, grinding valve seats and re-ringing pistons and how, when on a long run, the rider had to 'occasionally shut the throttle off, then open it up to oil the top end'. Less fondly he remembers the vibrations transmitted to the rider from springer forks when, returning from Phoenix almost non-stop, his hands began to swell alarmingly.

The first post-war Daytona 200 was run

in 1947, the same year as the AMA rally, races and Gypsy Tour in Hollister, California. This hitherto unremarkable event was about to become an indelible part of the history books. There are various accounts of the goings-on at Hollister over the weekend of 4 July 1947, which range from a full-scale riot to little more than general rowdiness and beer-drinking. The *San Francisco Chronicle* of 7 July describes it as 'The 40 hours that shook Hollister'. However, the boundaries between fact and fiction have become somewhat blurred by time and the fact that *Life* magazine and subsequently a moviemaker, Stanley Kramer, exploited the incident. Otherwise, even as the newsprint began to yellow, it would have slid into obscurity, and the beer-drinking, spinning

donuts, racing in the street and a few arrests for drunkenness regarded simply as 'boys having fun'.

However, the Columbia Pictures film, *The Wild One*, hit the screen in 1953. It starred Marlon Brando and Lee Marvin and, regardless of its interpretation of the facts, was seminal in a number of respects in that it set the style for future motorcyclists in terms of clothing and bikes. Brando, as the now legendary Johnny, wore a peaked cap and Highway Patrol jacket while Marvin, as his rival, was every inch the up-and-coming outlaw biker, complete with sleeveless jacket, scruffy beard, cap comforter and goggles. Brando's Johnny was the leader of the Black Rebels MC and rode a Triumph twin, while Marvin led the Beetles MC from the saddle

even though the machines were not in production in 1947.

The British bikes were seen as rivals to the two remaining American domestic manufacturers, Harley-Davidson and Indian, but were also regarded as a source of parts to be plundered for choppers. H.R. Kaye describes an early 74-ci (1200-cc) chopper in his book about the early days, *A Place in Hell*, though the period described is not quite certain: 'It was a masterpiece! The front fender had been removed and a Triumph front end installed. The rear fender was bobbed and chromed. It had dual headlights, apehangers, a custom tank and small leather saddle that had been pirated from an English racing machine. It had been painted black and polished to a blinding sheen. The

OPPOSITE LEFT
A bobbed big twin with solo seat and Flanders risers to raise the handlebars.

OPPOSITE RIGHT
This bobbed Panhead is officially known as a 'fatbob' because it retains the original gas tank.

LEFT and BELOW
Restored bobbers and vintage race bikes continue to draw a crowd at motorcycle events today.

of a chopped hog; it is an interesting fact that this is where the British pop group, The Beatles, got their name. So important was this film and the incident that was the start of it all, that in 1997 bikers returned to Hollister for the 50th anniversary of an event that is now an annual occurrence.

Apart from its effect on hundreds of youngsters, *The Wild One* also incurred the wrath of an America edging its way towards McCarthyism. The country had worries concerning destabilization and many took the film to be encouraging subversion and anti-social behaviour, seeing motorcyclists as no-good hoodlums, intent on disrupting American life. This opinion was widespread following the actual Hollister incident, and the American Motorcyclist Association,

keen to distance itself from what had happened, declared that while 99 per cent of all motorcyclists were upstanding citizens only the remainder was not. The Boozefighters had been one of the clubs present in Hollister at the time and was therefore maligned by this statement. Thus the One Percenters were born. Close examination of the photographs of Hollister at the time in the *San Francisco Chronicle* show pre-war big-twin Harleys with the front fenders removed, wide dresser bars on Flanders risers and at least one with a neatly bobbed rear fender cut back as far as the saddlebag hangers and fitted with a front fender trim. The telescopically-forked Harley, later seen in *The Wild One,* is treated similarly, creating this classic look

engine was clean and neat as a pin.'

The chopper in question was presumably a post-war Knucklehead, 74-ci variants of which were made in 1941 and from 1946–47, or a 1948 Panhead, these being the only years that 74 Harleys were made with springer forks. Had it already been fitted with telescopic forks there would have been little point in changing the front ends. It was called Mariah, after the wind.

Custom parts were few and far between but the earliest styles had been established, having made an appearance in bobbers and race-bikes of the forties and fifties. These early modified bikes defined the terminology of certain parts such as fatbob tanks. A bobber was a cut-down Harley but a fatbob was a cut-down Harley that had retained the wider stock two-piece tanks that the company utilized from 1936 onwards. Frame modifications started after the war with alterations to pre-war hill-climb frames and apehanger handlebars that were made from crash bars.

According to Wino Willie Forkner, in a

quote from the same 1986 interview, 'Before, hardly anybody except Harley made handlebars, we took Harley crash bars – because they were so damned tough and we didn't want them on the bikes anyway – and reshaped them. That's where the first hooks – you know, out, way up in the air, and down – apehangers they call them now – came from.' Other custom parts came from the K-model, introduced in 1952, and included the solo seat and the Sportster tank, the Sportster, having been introduced as the XL in 1957, becoming a perennial favourite. The rear fender was still a cut-down front fender, for the reason that it had no hinge but followed the correct radius for

OPPOSITE
This bobbed big-twin flathead has fishtail exhaust pipes and shortened rear fender.

LEFT and BELOW
Larry Pitts of New Jersey on his fifties Panhead chopper. The bike is fitted only with parts that were available during the fifties, including upswept fishtail pipes, apehangers and a Sparto tail light.

OPPOSITE and LEFT
Flathead Phil's 45-ci early-style chopper.
It features apehangers and a rear sissy
bar with integral rear fender struts but is
otherwise a stock Harley-Davidson with
a few modified parts. It features a 21in
(53-cm) diameter front wheel, Sportster
solo seat and a bobbed rear fender. The
bike also features the traditional hot-rod
black with flames paint job.

RIGHT
James Brusca (left) and Dan Hawkins from Pennsylvania, photographed at Daytona Bikeweek on their fifties-style choppers.

FAR RIGHT
Hawkins' bike features a small custom headlamp mounted on the standard headlamp bracket and a jockey shift (bottom right).

OPPOSITE
This big twin is period perfect and also has tall apehanger bars, upswept fishtail pipes, tiny pillion-pad rear seat and a bobbed rear fender.

PAGE 42
LEFT
James Brusca's Knucklehead is also a classic fifties chopper. It has black apehangers and a bobbed rear fender equipped with a Sparto tail light. It retains the stock gas tank and dash.

RIGHT
Brusca riding the chopper which has also had its front fender removed.

PAGE 43
The only non-original feature of this machine is its eye-catching leopard-skin paint job.

the diameter of the wheel. Another trick was to use the more minimal fenders from a British bike, especially those that were ribbed, which gave a considerably more sleek appearance to the big twins.

One of the few existing companies that actually made what can be termed custom parts, was that started by Lucile and Earl Flanders. Earl was a regular motorcycle competition rider who began to make custom

handlebars after the war for other competitors, bending the tube to suit his customers' requirements and manufacturing them to specific widths. Another product still bearing his name are Flanders risers, sometimes known as dog bones because of their shape, which are a pair of extension bars designed to lift the handlebars above the stock handlebar clamp.

'Stroker' motors became popular when

bars and chromed XA springer forks. These were taken from an experimental Second World War Harley-Davidson, the springers being 4in (10cm) longer than usual. The cast VL springers from pre-war big-twin flatheads were equally desirable for early choppers for similar reasons, and demonstrates how the mix-and-match concept of the chopper was firmly established from the very start.

In his book, *Hell's Angel*, published in 2000, Sonny Barger acknowledges that Hell's Angel choppers were born when the club 'started taking the front fenders off our bikes, cutting off the back fender and changing the handlebars'. He also makes the distinction between modifications made for functional reasons and those that are purely aesthetic: 'First we would take the windshields off, then throw out the saddlebags and switch the big old ugly seat with a smaller, skinny seat. We didn't need all of those lights either. We converted the oversized headlight to a smaller beam, replaced the straight handlebars with a set of high bars and replaced the bigger gas tanks with small teardrop-shaped tanks. We used old Mustang motorcycle gas tanks until the mid-fifties, when we started using narrow Sportster gas tanks. The tanks were changed for looks because the wide and thick stock tanks covered up the top of the motor. The design of the bank became radically streamlined, the curvature of the body narrow and sleek. It looked cooler if the front end was longer with a skinny front wheel. Plus you could see the whole motor, a real extra for a street machine.'

OPPOSITE, LEFT and ABOVE Recently, Chrome Specialties Inc. produced a modern version of a side-stick bobber. Its styling is true to the original but incorporates a few modern parts such as a front disc brake and a modern carburettor. Details such as the dice shifter knob and scallop paint scheme give it a fifties flavour.

mechanics began to realize that by mixing and matching Harley engine components it was possible to increase the capacity of a twin. A way of achieving this was to take the crankpin, flywheels and connecting rods out of the VL flathead and incorporate them into the later engines. The VL had a longer stroke than the overhead-valve engines and when used with the standard bore pistons increased the displacement without having to resort to expensive machining. The nickname is self-explanatory since, by increasing the engine's stroke, capacity was also increased.

Something happened in March 1948 that would later propel the chopper far beyond California's freeways, when the first chapter of the Hell's Angels was founded in Berdoo, San Bernardino, California, and by 1954 had become established in San Francisco. It is said that in order to found another chapter, a rider known as Rocky travelled north on a classic chopper of the time. It featured tall apehanger

CHAPTER TWO
THE SIXTIES:
PSYCHEDELIC CYCLES

There was a gradual evolution from the race-influenced bobber into the apehangered chopper. The process was imperceptible: it wasn't as though the clock stopped on one style before another began. Styles simply metamorphosed from one to the other in the manner of a kaleidoscope which, given the counter-culture, the summer of love and the climate of psychedelia that pervaded the sixties, is an appropriate analogy. George Wethern documented the early sixties in his 1979 book, *Wayward Angel*. 'In 1960, there were relatively few custom shops where dollars could be swapped for a sleek, chrome stallion. Grooming one yourself was the surest way to get a worthy mount.' He went on to describe the process thus: 'In addition to about $3,000 you needed mechanical know-how and energy to break down and refine a seventy-four-cubic-inch Harley-Davidson that rolled from the factory with doughnut tyres, a bulbous gas tank, heavy fenders and vanity size mirrors and an uninspiring paint job. We called them garbage wagons, but the 700-pound Harley stockers rolled like two-wheeled Cadillacs.'

It was clear that a stock Harley was regarded solely as the raw material from which a chopper would emerge. 'Behind the piggish profile was amazing power waiting to be freed with welding torches, wrenches and screwdrivers. With the cycle stripped to the bare frame, the engine was torn down, bored out to eighty cubic inches, pumped up in horsepower. A bicycle-sized twenty-one-inch front wheel was fitted to extended front forks that raked back the cut-down frame, the effect multiplied by riser handlebars with silver dollar sized mirrors. The fenders were thrown away or bobbed to the legal minimum. The cushy banana seat was thrown away and replaced with a lean saddle, the gas tank exchanged for a stinger with a twelve-coat finish of lacquer. Finally chrome pipes snorting the beast stood ready to buck with a chomp of metal gears.' The finished bike was

ABOVE
Another version of the popular hot-rod
flames theme is seen on this neatly-
chopped 45-ci flathead.

OPPOSITE
The extreme, spindly lines of choppers
are apparent in the silhouettes of these
two classic-style bikes.

acknowledged to be 200lb (90kg) lighter and therefore faster because of both the improved power to weight ratio and the tuned engine.

Freewheeling Frank, writing of the same era in 1967, defined a chopper in much the same terms and noted its origins as the particular choice of the One Percent. He wrote, 'A chopper means a Harley-Davidson motorcycle that has been stripped of extra accessories, including the fenders and tanks, which leaves only the frame and engine. These are then replaced with small fenders and one tank – along with straight pipes as the main changes. This leaves the motorcycle looking like a lean and furious monster. It's our creation, of our breed of horse. We love them.'

From 1948 to 1965 the Panhead was boss and its top-end clatter a familiar and beloved sound. The big V-twin motor looked at its best in a hardtail frame (i.e. Harley frames that predate the introduction of the Duo Glide). The looks of a rigid and a V-twin started it all, the only suspension being the 10-lb (4.5-kg) rear-tyre pressure; but the style was low, lean and clean. A perfect ride of the time consisted of the major components from the 74-ci (1200-cc) Harley-Davidson 'hog' and as little else as possible. Chopped hogs consisted of little more than the heavy Harley frame, forks and wheels, a 74-ci V-twin engine, small gas tank and tiny seat.

Much more recently Harley-Davidson registered the word HOG as an acronym for the Harley Owners Group. It then set about bringing litigation against all the chopper shops that had been using 'hog' in their name for decades. The irony of this is that although the company deliberately distanced itself from the One Percenters and their choppers it had frequently appropriated elements of their style as its own, to the extent of exploiting the notoriety of the past in advertising copy and equipping HOG members with back patches.

The increasing numbers of British bikes being imported into the U.S.A. meant that it was necessary to strip a Harley of its surplus parts as well as fitting dirt-track-type components and tuning the V-twin. This enabled the Harley to run on equal terms with the lighter British machines, whether it be on the track or from one stoplight to the next. Harley's XL Sportsters were specifically intended to compete with the

British imports. By the mid-sixties, however, the chopper had developed far beyond a stripped-down hog and was rapidly becoming a work of art.

The original idea of making modifications to improve the motorcycle's function was overtaken by those who made drastic changes to its form. Apehanger bars, bobbed fenders, small gas tanks and tiny seats were still *de rigueur*, but tall sissy bars, mini dual headlights, skinny front wheels, long mufflers that sometimes extended up the sides of the sissy bar and other such custom touches, were becoming more and more common, while chrome parts and custom-painted gas tanks were becoming increasingly popular. Sissy bars, so named because they prevented pillion passengers from falling off the rear of the machine, frequently extended to head height and were adorned with bayonets, swastikas or sculptured bar designs, as well as providing a place to mount the tail light and licence plate. In some places they are referred to as 'bitch bars' for obvious though uncomplimentary reasons.

Right or wrong, the sixties was the era of LSD and free love, of beautiful people and hippy happenings, of Allen Ginsberg and Ken Kesey, of protests against the Vietnam War. The U.S. Marine Corps was deployed in South Vietnam in 1965 as the U.S.A. assumed a full combat role in South East Asia. The late sixties, however, saw America bitterly divided over the issues surrounding the war, the belief in bikers and Hell's Angels as defenders of the counter-culture and guardians of the flower people having

OPPOSITE
Tall apehangers, tall sissy bar and long exhaust pipes: this classic Knucklehead chopper has it all.

LEFT
The Mustang gas tank from a moped of the same name became a popular custom fitment because its lines were sleeker than that of a stock Harley fatbob tank.

OPPOSITE and LEFT
Long forks and tall apehangers scream chopper. This is a 45-ci Harley-Davidson-powered machine based around a rigid custom frame and telescopic forks. It was built by Prof, seen here riding it.

RIGHT and OPPOSITE
This Texas-built Knucklehead features
extended stock springer forks and a
paint job influenced by Easy Rider. *It*
belongs to Dale and Martha, seen here
riding the bike in Greeley, Colorado.

been exposed as myths in the same year. A notable event was when the Oakland Hell's Angels interrupted an anti-war protest march from radical Berkeley to the army depot in Oakland. The truth of the matter was that bikers in the main tended to be blue collar in upbringing and outlook while the radical liberals were middle-class.

It was inevitable that the bikes of the sixties should reflect the psychedelic times in which they were conceived. Esoteric paint jobs and ever longer forks became the norm and a more definite style evolved. A radical chopper of the time featured a rigid frame, long forks – as often as not chromed springers – pullback bars, a sissy bar and a multi-hued paint job of sinuous swirls and twirls.

To accommodate the extended forks the frame rake needed to be altered. Alteration of the neck rake can have serious consequences for the handling characteristics of a motorcycle and was the subject of enormous scrutiny. It is almost impossible to generalize when it comes to altering the rake of a motorcycle front fork assembly, but it is an important concern for the builders and riders of choppers and those who regulate their construction and use. The two broad areas that need to be considered are handling and structure.

Consider the latter first: the question of structure hinges on whether the frame of the motorcycle is stiff enough to accommodate the forces exerted on it by any front fork assembly, the longer forks exerting different stresses on a frame. Whether a frame is adequate depends on the forces applied to the structure, the size and shape of the frame and

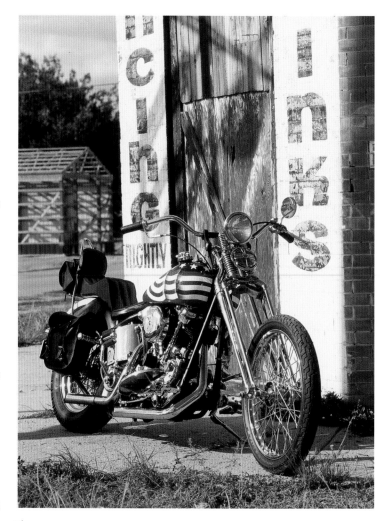

the materials from which it is assembled. All the forces applied to the forks and frame neck result from forces applied originally at the front wheel, be they constant or variable, constant forces being those such as weight of the machine, while variable ones are the ones generated by braking and turning.

Lengthening forks without physically altering the neck rake of the frame still alters the rake because of the additional length in the forks, it also changes the weight distribution of the whole motorcycle to the wheels; the longer the forks the less weight is supported by the front wheel, i.e. the constant load is reduced, although the centre of gravity stays almost constant in relation to the rear wheel.

Altering the neck rake of the motorcycle frame has similar effects and the steering neck loads also vary with wheelbase because of the torque applied. The load on the front wheel decreases as the load on the frame neck increases, due to the fact that the lever increases faster than the weight decreases as the wheelbase is lengthened. When the

OPPOSITE and BELOW
A particularly fine Panhead chop, where every component has been fitted with regards to the lines of the overall machine. The rear fender sits low to the tyre, the line of the frame runs straight from rear hub to headstock and so on.

RIGHT and OPPOSITE
This 1942 Knucklehead chop utilizes a
carefully chosen selection of original
Harley components and a few
aftermarket parts, such as the tall
apehangers, solo seat and pillion pad.
Its style may be old-school but its
purple-and-black flame paint job is
rather more modern.

motorcycle is moving, the forces applied to the front wheel increase rapidly when the wheel rolls over bumps. The forces applied vary both in terms of amount of force applied and the direction from which it is applied, including cornering and braking forces.

The rule of thumb is that cornering forces, when the machine is banked over to 45°, will increase the weight of bike and rider by around 40 per cent, while the neck torque will also be raised by 40 per cent independent of neck rake and extension. Braking loads are more dependent on wheelbase and in turn on both neck rake and extension. Braking with the rear wheel only some distance behind the centre of gravity gives rise to a torque action that results in an increased force on the front wheel and as the weight of the whole does not increase, there is less weight on the rear wheel. If the brakes are applied harder, the weight on the front wheel increases further and the weight on the rear decreases correspondingly. The next stage is that any further increase in torque through yet harder braking will cause the wheel to skid. When only one wheel is braked the torque caused will be less than when both are braked; the weight shift will be less as will braking force.

The actual percentages are affected by wheelbase so that an 85-in (2.16-m) wheelbase, for example, gives almost 60 per cent of the braking force of a two-wheel system, while on a machine with a stock wheelbase, only 45 per cent of the braking force can be supplied by the back brake. Structurally, the percentage of torque increase on the steering neck is most

OPPOSITE
Of all the stock bikes at Sturgis this
classic chopper was guaranteed to be a
headturner.

LEFT
A proud owner with his sixties-style
Knucklehead chopper at Daytona
Bikeweek.

important and in rear brake-only machines the percentage increase is dependent on wheelbase; when both brakes are used it is almost 60 per cent constantly. These figures mean that particularly long-wheelbased choppers with front and rear brakes need frame necks up to 90 per cent stronger than stock and rear brake-only bikes (which were,

and are, not legal everywhere) which need frame necks up to 70 per cent stronger than stock.

Loads that affect the steering neck must be transmitted to it by the forks and have a force versus compression characteristic inbuilt. In the case of springer and girder forks there is some kind of damping through

either friction or viscous damping; even the friction in the swivelling joints has some damping effect, but the front end needs to be constructed so that the springs are not bottomed out when the machine is static. The dynamic loading of the forks varies according to the direction from which the load is applied, something affected by rake,

the size of a bump and the speed at which it is hit.

Handling at various speeds is influenced by length of wheelbase as well as rake and trail. Rake is as described above and trail is the distance from an imaginary line down from the centre of the axle to where it intersects with an imaginary line down from the steering neck at the angle of the neck. A bike with a short wheelbase, short forks, small rake angle and correspondingly small trail will handle well at low speeds and be manoeuvrable. This makes it ideal, for example, for cross-country off-road use. Conversely, a bike with a longer wheelbase, bigger rake and therefore larger trail will be more stable at higher speeds. Drag bikes are an example of this extreme, with road bikes, race bikes and similar fitting somewhere in between. In choppers, the style is more important than the function, although the machine has to be rideable. As a result, many choppers are stable and comfortable at freeway speeds but less stable and manoeuvrable at low speeds. Adjusting the angle of the steering neck is one way to account for all of these factors and to accommodate longer forks.

In the late sixties a modification known as a gooseneck frame became popular, called this simply because the finished frame resembled a goose's neck. The frame top tube to the headstock was extended forward and the downtube was extended up and forward before the steering neck was refitted. This had the effect of lengthening the wheelbase and adjusting the neck to suit extended or aftermarket forks. Initially, springer forks were

popular for choppers and as aftermarket forks became commonly manufactured the problems of excessive trail could be eliminated through use of different lengths of rockers, i.e. the plates that connect both pairs of legs of the forks and carry the front axle. However, chopper builders soon came to the conclusion that frame necks required considerable strengthening for all but very small increases in wheelbase; rake and trail

OPPOSITE and ABOVE
This classic sixties-style chopper features a chain linkage for the foot-operated clutch lever as well as a small tank from a British bike of the period.

alterations could be mastered and as braking forces are not concentrated in the front wheel in long-wheelbased bikes, they were not as unmanageable or unsafe as some over-zealous traffic cops would claim.

Sonny Barger, in his book, *Hell's Angel*, reminisces about the sixties: 'Hell's Angels didn't buy a lot of parts. We made them. I made the first set of high bars I ever had from the chairs of those old chrome tables in the fifties with Formica tops. You'd get a set of those chairs and they were one inch thick and already bent. You'd cut off the two ends of the chair, and bang, you had a set of high bars.'

This dearth of custom parts meant that many companies came into being in the late sixties, including two in Minnesota: Smith Brothers & Fetrow of Minneapolis and Drag Specialties of Eden Prairie. There were others too, in 1969 Chicago Cycle Specialties of 2521 North Cicero Avenue, Chicago was advertising tubular gas and oil tanks, fork tube extensions, custom handlebars, seats and fenders and custom upswept exhausts. 'For show or go' there were pipes listed for 1947 and earlier and later (1948 and 1958) ohv suspension frames (Knuckles, Pans and Duo Glides) and XLCH Sportsters: with the exception of those for the Duo Glide, they retailed at $49.00 and extended way above the rider's head.

The fashion for extremely long forks has been mentioned by people like Von Dutch and others as evolving from the habit of using wide-angled lenses to photograph flamboyant bikes at custom shows. The lens made the forks look longer and builders ventured far beyond the XA springers in pursuit of this

OPPOSITE and LEFT
A classic chopper from Texas. This Knucklehead has been stripped of all the unnecessary stock parts and enhanced with exactly the right custom parts including tall apehangers, Sportster tank, solo seat, bobbed flat rear fender, Sparto tail light and a 21in diameter front wheel. It is perfection on wheels.

RIGHT
Fishtail exhaust pipes are so-named for
obvious reasons.

OPPOSITE
The small custom headlamp is generally
known as a Bates after its manufacturer.

look. Sonny Barger recalls making long springers when 'we took the rigid front end of one bike, cut it off, took another rigid, cut it off and welded them together to make the front end six inches longer. By extending the front end of the bike out, the frame dropped lower. Then we'd install the narrow fenders, grab rails and sissy bars. We made our own sissy bars and footpegs, moulding them out of metal, bending and welding them to our specifications. By the late-sixties and early-seventies, we might chop a bike to make it sit lower, but we didn't usually cut the frame. It only looked that way since our seats sat way back, right up on the rear fender'.

Across the bay from Oakland, the San Francisco chapter of the Hell's Angels developed the 'Frisco-mounted' tank. This involved putting the fuel tank – whether stock, Sportster or peanut – up on the top tube of the frame to make the engine more obvious. Frank Kozik, writing in *The Horse* magazine of September 2002 about Jimmy Souza, a Frisco Angel's bike, remarked that 'probably the most outstanding feature is a mid-fifties HD 125 Sprint tank which, according to Flash, was "better than gold" due to the trick, tank-mounted ignition and small size. The tank is mounted in a perfect Frisco-style suspended above and parallel to the top frame rail. One small problem, however, with this stylish system is that the extremely high tunnel in the Sprint tank, coupled with the upward angle of mounting, leaves the rider with only 0.75 of a gallon of usable fuel storage. But it does make for a perfect look'.

Ed 'Big Daddy' Roth built a variety of psychedelic machines, some of which were replicated in miniature by Revell, a maker of plastic kits. There were also the Mail Box and Candy Wagon trikes, which featured long springer forks with skinny front wheels and custom five-spoke car wheels on the rear axle. The Candy Wagon was based around a 45-ci (737-cc) GE model Servicar, while the Mail Box used a Crosley car engine. Both had fibreglass bodywork.

Cal, speaking in Danny Lyons' seminal book, *The Bikeriders*, touches on the motivation for building a chopper: 'You know what I dig man? I dig them beautifully customized jobs. You know why? 'Cause I look at a scooter, man, that's completely chopped, man, and every part on it he either made himself or bought special for it. Now you look at that dude, man, part of that scooter is him, man, and that dude's an outlaw. Whenever he rides, man, part of that scooter is him 'cause it's got his ideas and it's just him … But all choppers are different. Every one of 'em different. No matter how much alike you build. You know what I mean?' Further on he says, 'So when I look at a chopper, man, I respect the dude because he made his.'

Cal went on to describe his own chopper, a 1962 bike with a raked frame and a teardrop gas tank made from two Harley-Davidson tanks and moulded into the frame. Heavily detailed, it was painted in pearlescent colours with flames on the tank and a sword extending up the sissy bar. This approach to bike-building is confirmed by Keith Ball when he wrote that 'In the sixties the trimming process flourished with cutting torches and bondo'.

Possibly the biggest boost choppers ever had came in the last year of the decade when Columbia Pictures released *Easy Rider*, which, more than anything else, took the image of the chopper and the biker beyond the realms of California and its outlaw clubs and San Francisco's Haight-Ashbury circles. It wasn't the first of the biker movies, Kramer's *The Wild One* having had that distinction, and there had been others through the sixties, including *Wild Angels* and *Hell's Angels '69* and *Hell's Angels on Wheels*, which starred Jack Nicholson.

Easy Rider was not a big budget movie, in that it cost only $375,000 to make and would go on to gross more than $20 million for its distributors. It didn't have a complex plot, but simply followed Wyatt and Billy riding their choppers out on the road, but it captured mood, moment and movement to perfection. British Hell's Angel, Maz Harris, writing in 1985, recalls seeing the film: 'It was like drifting off into another world, a world which we desperately wished to experience for ourselves. In that single ninety-four minute budget movie, Dennis Hopper managed to encapsulate brilliantly the very spirit of freedom that we had all felt, at one time or another, out there on the road. He presented on screen a ceremonial vindication of what we'd known all along but were unable to articulate.'

The film follows two enigmatic characters, Wyatt, played by Peter Fonda, and Billy, played by Dennis Hopper, as they proceed cross-country aboard two Harley choppers. The film gives no clue as to their past lives, it not being where they've come

from but where they are going that is important. Their ultimate destination is the Mardi Gras in New Orleans but it could be anywhere. They are, as the Steppenwolf theme song says, 'looking for adventure and whatever comes our way'.

The film is set in uncertain times during the Vietnam War, while American forces are engaged in a desperate struggle for Hill 937, Hamburger Hill, east of the Laotian border, at the time of its release. The film underlines the conflicts within America's changing society and almost inevitably ends in tragedy. The couple's one-and-only companion on the road, George, a whiskey-drinking lawyer, played by Jack Nicholson, is murdered, as too, eventually are Wyatt and Billy. However, the tragic ending does nothing to alter the effect the film and suddenly bikers everywhere were 'looking for themselves' from the saddles of choppers. Another effect of the movie was that it spread the word abroad, popularizing choppers notably in Australia and Europe.

The choppers in the film were completely typical of the time: both of the characters ride Panhead choppers, although they differ in style. Fonda's bike, *Captain America*, is a wishbone rigid-framed bike with an overstock telescopic front end. Apehanger bars are mounted on risers, there is no front brake or fender, but a Mustang tank, dual seat and tall sissy bar are fitted and the chopper is finished with a stars and stripes paint job. Hopper's is decorated with flames: it too features a wishbone frame and Mustang tank but the forks are not as long or as raked and have T-bars bolted to the top

yoke. The bike has a small, English-style front fender and the stock drum brake.

These are the machines that launched a style that irrevocably linked choppers and long forks together. Fashion being what it is, while both bikes would still be welcome at any custom bike event, Fonda's looks like a late-sixties/early-seventies chopper while Hopper's slightly more restrained bike hasn't really ever gone out of style, with the possible exception of the handlebars. So famous have these machines become that *Easyriders* magazine built replicas for display purposes, the replica *Captain America* bike being included in this book (see pages 46 and 47). As a result of that movie, rigid frames and high bars are as much a part of motorcycling for many as

highways and Harleys. Stephen Dalton, reviewing *Easy Rider* for *The Times* in September 2004 wrote, 'This landmark in hippie biker movies changed the face of cinema, bringing druggy counter-culture chic to a mainstream audience. It co-stars the director Dennis Hopper, Peter Fonda and Jack Nicholson in his breakthrough role. Viewed with three decades of hindsight, *Easy Rider* actually seems much less about celebrating hippie-era values and much more about eulogizing some elusive, Old West ideal of American freedom. Perhaps the saddest legacy is a long-running authorship dispute between Hopper and the screenwriter Terry Southern, which still rumbles on despite Southern's death in 1995.'

OPPOSITE
A classic Panhead chopper with a custom gas tank, neatly modified and moulded rear fender and a tombstone tail light. The stock-length forks have been slightly raked.

BELOW LEFT
Fitting a mini-speedo alongside the engine is one way of facilitating the removal of the stock two-piece fatbob tank with its tank-mounted dash and speedo.

CHAPTER THREE
THE SEVENTIES:
THE TIMES THEY ARE A-CHANGING

Hell's Angel Sonny Barger's idea of the chopper is insightful, as befits a man whose role in One Percenter motorcycling is pivotal. In *Hell's Angel*, he writes that 'we

designed and built a bike that ran damn smooth, using the least amount of parts and accessories. Choppers were stripped down for speed, looks and ultimate discomfort.

After we got through with them they weren't the easiest bikes to ride, but what the hell, at least we looked cool. It became a style and a look: a bitch bar [sissy bar] so your chick could lay back. When we'd ride down the street, people would check us out – and that was what it was all about'. These were wild bikes, and Harley-Davidson finally acknowledged their existence in 1970.

In that year, the company launched the Super Glide, which *Cycle* magazine put on the cover of its November 1970 issue. Inside it said: 'The members of the Harley-Davidson styling team, in response to the genius of Dick Hirschberg, the impact of the chopper phenomenon, and the success of *Easy Rider*, have savaged the venerable Electra Glide like tigers at a goat and herewith present to you the ... Super Glide, Sonnet on Extravagance.'

How had the transition of this machine from a Milwaukee drawing board and onto the street been achieved? According to *Cycle*, when it asked William G. Davidson, Harley-Davidson's styling chief, it was 'the influence of the California bob-jobs; not full choppers as such, but lightened, leaned-down

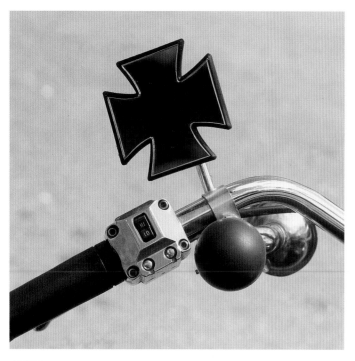

ABOVE
Maltese-cross mirrors and vintage-style horns were popular custom parts in the seventies.

ABOVE RIGHT
Largely for show, these custom forks did offer some suspension but it would have been minimal.

bikes that were recognizable as 74s'.

The Super Glide was launched with a red-white-and-blue paint job, but despite the obvious parallel with Fonda's bike in *Easy Rider*, the manufacturer was keen to distance itself from the whole chopper scene. Davidson also had this to say: 'As a company we're leery of the chopper image and any kind of extremism.' However, in a 1999 book entitled *Outlaw Machine*, Brock Yates saw the Super Glide as the answer to

the two-fold challenge that faced Harley-Davidson. The company realized it must capitalize on the raffish image it had acquired as a result of Hollister, the Hell's Angels and *Easy Rider*, while competing with the squeaky-clean Japanese high-performance café racers.

Yates thought that 'Davidson's solution was to cobble together pieces from the monstrous dressers and the lighter Sportsters in a daring combination. The big twin's

engine, frame and rear suspension were mated to the smaller bike's fuel tank, slightly extended front forks and zoomy fibreglass seat and tail. Davidson then took a radical leap backward by eliminating the electric start to reduce weight. This was an open acknowledgement of the chopper riders who had long favoured the older, more basic Harleys and their ancient kick-starters. Davidson's final gesture was to paint the motorcycle in garish red, white and blue, a

clear paean to the confused patriotic themes swirling through the nation at the time.'

It was an uncertain period for the stars and stripes because times were changing fast; while protesters were burning the flag, others still stood up. President Nixon had been inaugurated in 1969 and had taken a completely different approach to the Vietnam War, his scaling down of U.S. military involvement being one aspect of this. Despite the ongoing controversy about Vietnam, dealers were clearly aware who their customers were; in fact, in 1970, advertisements for Dudley Perkins Co., a San Francisco dealer since 1914, included a line that read, 'Returning Servicemen Welcome'.

Around at that time was a shop called Two-Wheelers, run by Arlin Fatland, a member of the Hamsters MC who had been riding and building customs for the best part of 30 years. He had actually been a founder member of the Hamsters and still runs Two-Wheelers in Denver as an independent bike shop on the same site where it has been since 1970. Back then it was a small establishment servicing, repairing and building bikes, selling clothing and accessories and facing tough times.

The AMF-era Harleys weren't too spectacular so not everyone wanted them, but they did ensure the workshop was fully occupied. Things got tougher in other ways: Two-Wheelers is situated on the corner of 38th and Navajo in a largely Hispanic neighbourhood. Not long after the shop opened a bunch of Hispanic heavies suggested that bikers were not welcome in the neighbourhood, but bikers being bikers

Tall sissy bars often incorporated fender struts and licence plates, while Maltese-cross tail lights were another popular accessory.

OPPOSITE and THIS PAGE
Excessively garish choppers, such as this
Sportster-powered machine, are typical
of the seventies. The bike has had
endless money, time and chrome lavished
on it but the overall appearance is over-
cluttered and not particularly sleek.

they were not so easily intimidated; but it is
still possible to see the bullet holes in the wall
outside the shop. In these 34 years the shop
has built some of America's most
photographed custom bikes and become a
major landmark in its own right; in fact, at one
time or another most custom magazines have
carried a feature on Arlin's work.

Harley-Davidson introduced its refined
overhead-valve 74-ci engine in 1966 and it
quickly became known as the Shovelhead – a
nickname that is now universal, which arose
because the rocker covers look like the backs
of upturned shovels. This engine was used in
the Super Glide, without doubt the factory's
interpretation of a custom bike. Harley had
taken an FL Electra Glide, removed the

cumbersome front end and replaced it with
the lighter one from an XL Sportster – hence
its FX designation. It had fitted a 3.5-gallon
fatbob tank and a custom-style dual seat unit
with an integral tail light. Amid talk of the
lack of frame flex, of rake and trail and
cornering, *Cycle* magazine remarked that
'Everybody likes it; everybody has to like it
for one reason or another'. It went on to
predict that the Super Glide would succeed
like no other motorcycle the company had
ever built, and it was right; the Super Glide
has been in Harley's range ever since and the
concept of the factory custom was proven
beyond all doubt. Subsequently, most of the
world's major motorcycle manufacturers
have at one time or another included factory
customs in their range.

In the same issue of *Cycle* magazine,
which followed its test of the new Super
Glide, Routt's Cycle Center Inc. of
Hyattsville, Maryland was advertising
extended forks, fork braces, bolt-on rigid
rear-frame sections and custom seats. With
the exception of the forks, all were advertised
for British bikes and Harleys, though the fork
tubes were also available for Hondas. The
seventies would see a burgeoning market in
choppers powered by engines other than
those of Harley-Davidson manufacture. This
was partially because of the availability and
cheapness of these other makes of
motorcycle, especially those from British and
Japanese manufacturers.

Despite this, many of the so-called
custom components used in their
construction owed their origin to Harley-
Davidson. Fatbob and Sportster tanks are

OPPOSITE
A restrained street-ridden Sportster
chopper fitted with springer forks,
pullback bars and a short sissy bar.

LEFT
A definitive seventies chopper – long
springer forks, no front brake and tall
pipes – illuminated by the lights of
surrounding buildings.

RIGHT
A New Old Stock (NOS) seventies custom part still in the box at a swap meet. In this case it is one of the once popular Maltese cross tail lights.

FAR RIGHT
Custom seventies springers were designed along similar lines to Harley-Davidson's original springer forks but with more slender tubes and more angular yokes.

OPPOSITE
Harley Sportsters were a popular choice of bike to chop during the seventies because their compact, unit-construction engines allowed the fabrication of a long, narrow bike – especially when springer forks were fitted, as this example photographed at Daytona Bikeweek illustrates.

PAGE 82
A Sportster chopper with long springer forks and the traditional flame paint job.

PAGE 83
A long, springer-forked chopper based around a Shovelhead engine. It has a prism tank, something else popular in the seventies.

obvious examples as well as springer forks and rigid frames, the like of which had never been used by Honda, as well as specific items such as tombstone tail lights that were stock Harley items between 1946 and 1954.

It is equally true to say that Maltese cross tail lights, prism tanks and tall sissy bars are custom items designed specifically for choppers, regardless of their engine type. The tradition of building choppers powered by engines other than Harleys endures: in Great Britain there is a long tradition of building 'specials', which began with café racer Tritons – a combination of Norton cycle parts and a Triumph Twin engine.

In Europe, Harley-Davidsons were not at all plentiful, with the exception of military surplus WLA and WLC models, so in the early seventies European choppers were frequently based around these as well as various British and Japanese motorcycle engines. The Triumph Twin and Honda Four engines were both popular choices.

In 1972 chopper parts were being advertised by a number of Californian companies, including D&D Distributors of Burbank, Eyeball Engineering of Rialto, Mother's Choppers of Anaheim, Paughco of North Hollywood, Durfee of Stanton and Vista Chopper Products of Glendale. Of

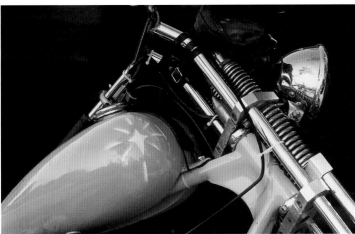

these, D&D, Eyeball, Mother's, Durfee and Paughco offered long front ends alongside other products.

Besides these, there were many more in business in the U.S. or about to be, including Arlen Ness, Gary Bang, Denver's Choppers, Bay Area Custom Cycles, American Motorcycle Engineering, B.C. Choppers, C&G Manufacturing, Santee, P&P, SIE, Hallcraft, Invader, Chopper Corner, HR Custom Choppers, GME, Tom's Accessories Inc., Cycle Saloon Inc., Allied, Jardine, T&S, Pucketts, Cycles International, Hill Engineering, Ed's Chopper Parts, Cycle Parts Unlimited, B&R products, Michigan Motorcycle Accessories, Red Rider, Expert Cycle, Cycle Seats, California Choppers, Two-Wheelers of Denver, Custom Cycle

OPPOSITE and THIS PAGE
A classic seventies Panhead chopper that features numerous custom parts. It is based around an aftermarket frame, custom springer forks, five-spoke chromed steel wheels and a Mustang tank. Only the engine and transmission were probably made by Harley-Davidson and even the engine has an aftermarket SU carburettor conversion fitted.

ABOVE
Angular gas tanks, chromed girder forks and stepped king and queen seats were all popular seventies custom parts and all can be seen on this rigid Panhead.

OPPOSITE
A very low Sportster-engined rigid chop with springer forks, custom gas tank, bobbed rear fender and upswept fishtail pipes. The sissy bar is also the rear fender strut and spoked wheels complete the state-of-the-art late-seventies look.

Delight Inc., Forking by Frank, D&K, Cycle Supply and more.

Parts were being designed and created all the time. John Flanders of the Flanders company was on the road selling to motorcycle shops, ready for when the guys at Cheat'ah Choppers of 3500 W.Westminster Boulevard in Santa Ana, California, asked for a specific design of handlebar that would bend right back. This became known as the 'California Pullback' and within months became Flanders' top-selling handlebar of the seventies. There was another similar design that was referred to as a 'six-bend pullback'

because the design incorporated six bends in the tubing. Such was the enthusiasm for chopper building that an Illinois-based company called SIE, which advertised itself as the nation's largest distributor of custom parts and claimed to 'ride what we sell', offered franchises to would-be chopper-shop proprietors on a $2,500 minimum franchise.

Other custom components increased in popularity and gas tanks shaped like small coffins, prisms and diamonds all appeared in advertisements and, more importantly, on bikes. Seats soon rose to the full height of

sissy bars, with seats stepped by 6in (15cm) or more becoming known as king and queen seats. Disc brake conversions, plunger frames custom exhausts and hexagonal- and octagonal-section oil tanks were all being manufactured.

Highway pegs were another custom component and allowed the rider's feet to be placed further forward of the normal riding position and to ride with legs outstretched – hence their name. Such pegs complemented the upright riding position of the chopper as compared to a stock bike. The style of custom paintwork also progressed through the seventies, with graphics gaining popularity and often incorporating panels of metalflake paint. Murals portraying any number of scenes became fashionable and were painstakingly applied by airbrush specialists. Popular themes for these included dragons, snakes and mythical creatures in fantasy scenes, as well as naked and partially-clothed women. Perennially popular designs and variations on flames and skulls also evolved in parallel with the newer styles.

As the popularity of choppers increased exponentially a number of enthusiast magazines also made an appearance, such as *Chopper, Street Chopper* and *Custom Chopper* in 1970, followed by *Easyriders* in June 1971. While several came and went, others went from strength to strength, including *Easyriders*, which is still published to this day, while *Street Chopper* evolved into *Hot Bike*, a magazine which is still available, and *Iron Horse* was a spin-off from *Easyriders*. Their difference from the mainstream magazines is indicated by Brock

OPPOSITE
This Sportster was built in Colorado in 1976 around a plunger frame. It is almost rigid but has a spring-mounted rear axle that offers a degree of rear suspension. Little is left of the original Sportster apart from the engine, with wheels, girder forks, seat, gas tank and handlebars all being custom parts.

LEFT
This would have been a head-turning bike when it was first completed, as prism tanks and gaudy paintwork were both seventies favourites.

The plunger frame was a seventies favourite and many, known as Saviors, were manufactured by AMEN, an acronym of American Motorcycle Engineering.

highly regarded was the Jammer's Handbook. Mil Blair was the man behind D&D but later changed the company name to Jammer Cycle and with Joe Teresi and Lou Kimzey produced a series of Jammer's Handbooks. These were a combination of feature bikes, technical features and parts catalogue, offering parts for Harleys, British and Japanese bikes and were published annually. As early as 1975, Jammer Cycle Products was able to state the following in its advertising: 'We've been around a long time – since back when chopper was a dirty word – and we plan on being around for a long time to come'. This indictes how reviled choppers had once been. Jammer remained in business until 1993 and it is hard to

Yates, writing in *Outlaw Machine*. 'Speaking directly to the biker crowd, monthlies like *Easyriders* and *Iron Horse* featured tattooed, bare-breasted bimbos sprawled on custom Harleys in open defiance of the pie-faced imagery being peddled by the manufacturer.'

The specific chopper magazines were the first regular publications to chronicle the development of ideas and trends within chopper-building circles. The widespread U.S. and international distribution also meant that fashions would no longer remain localized. From the pages of a magazine it was possible, by looking closely at featured bikes, reading how-to features and obtaining mail-order parts from advertisers, to build a chopper almost anywhere.

Another publication that came to be

OPPOSITE RIGHT
Chopper magazines, like those in this
selection, carried advertisements for
mail-order parts, which meant that
choppers could be built anywhere.

LEFT
Important seventies touches are all
present on these Panheads, including
extended telescopic forks, tall back rests
on sissy bars and twin rectangular
headlights.

underestimate the influence of its handbooks on chopper builders, simply through making parts available; in 1976, for example, the company reprinted its first three handbooks as a 160-page volume in which it listed 2,000 product lines.

When one looks at the magazines of the seventies, it is immediately evident that the desire to be different was what mattered most: some choppers were completely over the top with every feature taken to excess, especially in show-bike circles, the relative purity of what had gone before being practically non-existent – even psychedelia had become mainstream by the mid-seventies. With hindsight, it would appear that other components appear ugly as a result of the limited manufacturing technology then available, especially where new technology existed but could not be applied sufficiently well to retain the graceful lines of older-style parts; however, these parts were considered avant-garde at the time.

Square-section girder forks, candy-twist steel springer forks, spoked Invader wheels, that were assembled with a minimal number of square-section tubular spokes, were all fashionable items but would now be considered dated. Many of the smaller chopper components were tacky, including Maltese cross mirrors and tail lights, Nazi eagle tail lights and tall sissy bars that incorporated bayonets, swastikas or peace signs. The fashion for swastikas and Iron Crosses emanated from the One Percenters, who sported Second World War memorabilia to shock the 'citizens', as they disparagingly called the non-biking public. It invariably

OPPOSITE
A chopped flathead with long custom springers, Sportster tank and a rigid frame – simple but effective.

LEFT
Long girder forks, like the ones fitted to this chopper, offer suspension via a spring mechanism near the bike's headstock.

worked, though elements of white power did
infiltrate the biker community later on, as
happens in any other large segment of
society drawn from varying backgrounds.

There were, of course, many exceptions
to the lack of taste apparent in some
seventies chopper components and it was
possible to build a righteous ride. With the
benefit of more than two decades of
hindsight, it is clear that the choppers that do
not appear gaudy and tasteless, even though
they are clearly dated, are those that have
long flowing lines rather than clumsy angular
ones. Two distinct styles evolved: as well as
choppers with long forks, a long, low, super-
extended bike became popular in the San
Francisco Bay Area during the early
seventies.

The style was developed by Arlen Ness,
Ron Simms and others in northern California
and became popular all over the U.S.A. and
beyond. By the mid-seventies there were two
distinct styles: the low-slung look
popularized by builders such as Denver's
Choppers and the Nor-Cal Frisco Ness style.
The latter was based around short front ends,
diamond tanks, drag bars and strutted tails.
Of these main components, diamond gas
tanks were of faceted steel, drag bars were
almost straight and flat handlebars and
strutted tails were in swing-arm frames, the
shock absorbers replaced by chromed steel
struts which effectively made them rigid, the
length of the strut determining how low the
bike would ride.

Many of these low riders and diggers
used Sportster engines because it was
possible to build a slimmer bike than if the

RIGHT
A long and low Panhead chopper. The type of springers fitted are known as candy-twist because of the type of steel used in their construction.

OPPOSITE
A girder-forked Sportster chopper on the beach at Daytona. Note the tine front disc brake.

PAGE 98
An extreme rigid Shovelhead chopper with springer fork. Note how flames have been incorporated into the frame gusset under the tank.

PAGE 99
A rat chopper based on a Sportster at Daytona Beach.

The second style of chopper prevalent in the seventies was the rigid-framed machine with long forks, a small gas tank on the top tube, long pullback bars, possibly a tall sissy bar, and a stepped seat. On both styles the tank and frame were often moulded and angles smoothed out with bondo, while show bikes of both kinds featured sculptured components. Some components went far beyond what was practical, one such item being rigid forks. These were simply chromed tubes and while they made a chopper's front end look clean and uncluttered they would not have enhanced handling; the only suspension they offered was in the flexing of the tubes.

As anti-heroes, chopper-riding bikers had few equals at this time. The so-called biker exploitation movies and salacious newspaper coverage ensured their wholesale vilification, to the extent that when a movie or book

Two approaches to chopping a Sportster: the rat bike (above) based on modified standard components and (right) one of Arlen Ness' show-stopping Bay Area Low Riders.

bigger 74-ci Harley V-twin engine had been used. Certain components were designed especially for these bikes, the hardhead frame and Bay Area springers being just two examples. The hardhead was a section of frame that incorporated a steering head that required welding into a stock frame and had the effect of both altering the rake and lengthening the frame. Bay Area springers were a slender version of Harley's springer forks that enhanced the slim, almost delicate, lines of such bikes. A third component, designed for these low riders, was a glass-fibre rear fender designed by Arlen Ness. It was minimal but incorporated a mounting for the rear light.

called for bad guys, they were frequently bikers. An example of this is contained in *The Gauntlet*, a Clint Eastwood cop movie. To set the scene, the novel of the screenplay, by Michael Butler and Dennis Shyrack, includes the following: 'There were tents, gear, tools, women and children – all assembled around a scattered core of some fifty customized bikes. The bearded, dirty, Viking-like men were either sitting listlessly on the ground with their mommas or straddling their hogs, arms outstretched to the handlebars, hands twitching on the throttles, scraggly heads nodding to the ululating cadence of the machines.'

The bikers are fair game, people whose bikes can be stolen with impunity and who can ultimately be shot; moreover, the authors can't resist allowing Ben Shockley

LEFT
Prism tanks lent themselves to panelled custom paintwork.

BELOW
A performance-inspired Bay Area Low Rider from Arlen Ness.

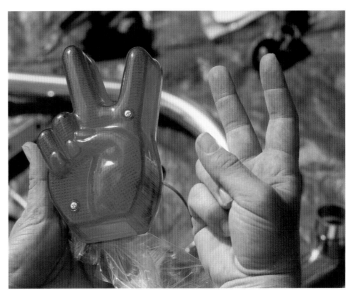

(Eastwood's character) to enjoy his ride on a stolen chopper: 'By the time they'd reached the highway, Ben found himself relaxing astride the noisy chopper … remembering those feelings of freedom and independence Ben wished he could feel them again.' *Clint Eastwood, All American Anti-Hero*, a book published in 1977, immediately before the release of *The Gauntlet* remarks that 'one suspects that Eastwood has little understanding of, or sympathy for, that large part of American youth which has been characterized as an "alternative culture". In all his modern-day films youth received something of a raw deal.' Holding up an outlaw bike club with a .44 Magnum in *The*

OPPOSITE
Generator Shovelhead, its original frame modified with raked-out headstock.

ABOVE LEFT and ABOVE
The peace sign tail light was a custom accessory available during the seventies. This is a NOS item seen at a swap meet.

LEFT
A low rigid Sportster with custom girder forks.

OPPOSITE
For some, the period of the seventies was all about excess: note the heavily modified and moulded frame and rear fender.

FAR LEFT
Long custom springers and apehangers are still in evidence on the streets of Daytona and Sturgis.

LEFT
A subtler moulding job, this Sportster tank has been moulded into the frame in front of the seat.

Gauntlet suggests that nothing had changed. Indeed later Eastwood movies – *Any Which Way but Loose* and its sequel – ridiculed a fictitious chopper-riding outlaw club.

Because of the informal nature of the chopper-rider's world and the casual way choppers have evolved and new styles in

fashions develop, it isn't possible to pinpoint exact dates when a particular type of chopper ceased to be built. In general, there is more of a gradual shift from one style to another so that, for example, the distinction between the late-sixties and early-seventies is somewhat blurred. However, it is possible to differentiate, at a glance, between bikes from opposite ends of the decade, despite the ever-evolving process. External factors, including the changing motorcycle market in the U.S.A., were also responsible for this.

After a considerable amount of negotiation, AMF (American Machine and Foundry), a huge conglomerate owning a

OPPOSITE
This Bay Area Low Rider has custom springers made by Arlen Ness, a prism tank and struts that convert the swing-arm frame into a rigid by replacing the shock absorbers.

LEFT and ABOVE
The key to chopping bikes is to get the lines right in order to achieve a comfortable riding position with feet forward and arms outstretched, as demonstrated here.

of the factory Super Glide models which would influence the styles of choppers to come.

Choppers began to seriously diversify in the mid-seventies: as well as the various low rider and long-forked styles, there was a less obvious but possibly more important divergence. Show bikes were becoming less and less like rideable street bikes and ever more extravagant, so a style of chopper began to emerge designed for riding. The successful formula incorporated a mixture of factory-manufactured Harley parts, such as engine, transmission and maybe the forks and frame, with a combination of custom parts from companies such as Jammer and Paughco providing tank, frame, forks and

PAGES 108 and 109
Two approaches to chopping a seventies Panhead: candy-twist springers and five-spoked wheel and chromed girders and laced wheel.

OPPOSITE
One girl and her bike.

LEFT and BELOW
Varying styles of big-twin springer choppers: a Shovelhead in a custom rigid frame with a prism tank and a disc front brake and a Panhead with a stepped dual seat, a peanut tank and a drum brake.

variety of leisure and industrial companies took control of Harley-Davidson on 7 January 1969, but it was not an entirely happy marriage and led to a strike over job losses, problems with quality control and all the other symptoms of a dissatisfied workforce. In spite of this, however, the early seventies were boom years for motorcycle sales and the AMF-controlled company managed to increase production enormously. In the long term this was to compound the problems of quality control, which was not immediately evident. AMF is frequently criticized for its management of Harley-Davidson, but it is generally accepted that if

it had not bought Harley-Davidson when it did, the company would not have survived.

The seventies was the era of the new generation of Japanese superbikes and AMF began to consider withdrawing from the Harley-Davidson operation. As the decade progressed, the percentage share of the market enjoyed by Harley-Davidson was declining in the face of ever-increasing numbers of oriental imports to the U.S.A. Unreliable quality meant that Harleys were only bought by the dedicated few and in many cases the factory bikes were seen for what they could be rather than for what they were. This was compounded by the success

RIGHT
Pigpen with his radical seventies-style chopper at Steamboat Springs, Colorado. It is based around a Panhead, and has a number of angular parts as well as girder forks.

OPPOSITE
This seventies-style Sportster chopper utilizes a plunger frame and extended standard telescopic forks with a variety of custom parts to give a long, low look.

ABOVE
A drag bike-styled seventies custom.

RIGHT
Minimal suspension is offered by this custom plunger frame.

OPPOSITE
Two-up on a rigid Shovelhead chopper seen at Daytona.

saddle. The resulting custom bikes were usually Panhead- or Shovelhead-powered choppers using rigid or swing-arm frames and telescopic or springer forks. When finished with a combination of smaller parts from either custom suppliers or OEM, considerable diversity of appearance and detail could be achieved, albeit as variations of a general style.

In 1979, as the decade drew to a close, Drag Specialties was supplying many of the custom components to build chopped Harleys. In its advertisements, it claimed to be the premier motorcycle accessory supplier, with over 9,000 dealers worldwide. In the same year Jammer was offering items such as belt primary drive conversions and stamped-steel custom wheels that bolted to a

OPPOSITE
A standard rigid Shovelhead chopper on show at Daytona.

LEFT
This street-ridden Sportster chopper has a disc-braked springer front end.

RIGHT
A Sportster chopper, with girder forks, twin disc front brake, cast-alloy wheels and T-bars, is a combination of stock and custom parts.

OPPOSITE
Arlin Fatland's Sportster low rider incorporates a prism tank, gold-leaf paintwork and gold plating, as well as slender custom springer forks. Fatland described it as handling like a barrow full of wet cement.

hub assembly (in later years this type of wheel would be machined from billet alloy). The overall style of the rideable chopper was reflected in the factory's successful Super Glide models. These, in their component form, comprised a Shovelhead engine in a swing-arm frame, with a telescopic front end, minimal fenders and other cycle parts. This combination of parts was achievable by using an AMF Harley and a number of custom components.

Various FX models were manufactured and sold throughout the seventies, including the decidedly custom-looking FXS Low Rider of 1977. This machine incorporated shorter forks with greater rake, cast wheels and a fatbob gas tank. A crinkle-finish black Shovelhead engine and silver-painted tank and fenders completed the custom look.

With ersatz choppers rolling off the factory's assembly lines and selling from dealers' showroom floors the chopper entered the eighties with something of an identity crisis. Brock Yates wrote of the era and the annual pilgrimage to Sturgis thus: 'For much of August the interstates of Wyoming and the Dakotas swarmed with Harleys, most of them snorting choppers ridden by authentic bikers, the One Percenters, their bedrolls and sometimes their old ladies [riding 'sissy'] mounted behind them. Sturgis was the real thing legitimized and commercialized by the appearance of corporate types like Willie G. Davidson and the use of the Sturgis name for the all-black, belt-drive FXDB in 1980.'

CHAPTER FOUR
THE EIGHTIES:
AGAINST THE WIND

For 1981 AMF Harley-Davidson decided to take the concept of the factory custom a great deal further by announcing the FXWG. This was an FX Super Glide with a Wide Glide front end, hence its WG suffix. It was, Harley claimed, 'the only factory-built custom in sight' and featured a 21-in (53-cm) front wheel and 16-in (41-cm) rear, extended front forks with Electra Glide sliders, staggered short dual pipes and a bobbed rear fender. To round off the custom appearance the FXWG was available with a flame paint job over black or in four different metallic colours.

For years, Harley dealers had been feathering their own nests by marketing unofficial aftermarket parts, but now the factory was beginning to offer its own choppers as well as ranges of aftermarket custom parts. There was still a market for the independent manufacturers, of course, despite the downturn in the U.S. economy in the early eighties. The aftermarket products being manufactured and distributed for Harleys and advertised in the specialist magazines included components from Drag Specialties, Graves Plating, Performance

Machine Inc., Jammer Cycle Products, Righteous Products, Brown's Plating, Lonesome MFG, Two-Wheelers M/C Shop of Denver, Paramount Speedometer, Forking by Frank, C&G Mfg. Co., Paughco, Allied Distributing & Mfg. Inc., Bay Area Custom Cycles, AMEN, Phase 3, Denver's Choppers, Elite Corporation, Smith Brothers & Fetrow Inc., Custom Cycle Delight Inc., Truett & Osborn, Arlen Ness, Expert Cycle Inc., Routt's Cycle, S&S, Nostalgia Cycle, P&P Distributors, Santee, Speed & Cycle Shop Inc., Cycle Fabrications, California Cycle Works, SIE Inc., FuBaR, Chopper Specialties, Sugar Bear's Chop Shop and in some publications AMF Harley-Davidson itself. When one compares this with the similar list in Chapter three, it is surprising how many of them were in business ten years earlier.

Among the products of these companies

OPPOSITE
Ken Schulz's chopped FX Shovelhead.

ABOVE
A rigid Shovelhead with springers and Sportster tank on Daytona Beach.

OPPOSITE
The Super Glide, Harley-Davidson's take
on the chopper.

LEFT
This is how many modified Shovelheads
looked during the eighties.

were items upgraded to suit more modern components, such as the Smith Brothers & Fetrow square-section girder forks designed to accept single or twin Harley brake discs and calipers as well as the stock cast wheels. AMEN (American Motorcycle Engineering) offered the Savior frame that featured plunger-type rear suspension, which was intended to offer some rear suspension but with most of the looks of a rigid frame.

Street Chopper magazine produced a series of five guides to help builders get their choppers up and running. It dealt with frame and tank modifications, chopper electrics, custom wheels and front ends, building one's own trike and chopper styling. Times were changing, however: Gary Bang, involved in the custom parts business since its earliest days, was interviewed by *Easyriders* magazine in 1987 and indicated the fickleness of fashion when he remarked: 'We were tired of the 2.2 gallon tank, it was a style that we were tired of, absolutely tired of, just like we were tired of bell-bottom pants. Along came the gas crunch. Boy, we needed more gas. Everybody knew that. What to do? They tried making the tank

THIS PAGE and OPPOSITE
Chopped Panheads: extended forks with front fender (above) and Wide Glide front end without a fender (right and opposite) – typical of many eighties street-ridden choppers.

bigger, but it got uglier. Then they said, "let's put fatbobs back on". We took fatbobs off in the '60s and threw them in the trash and now those same fatbob tanks, speedos and dashes are worth $250 a unit. So we did the fatbobs. But when we did them the front ends came lower, 'cause the tanks didn't look right up there. More fenders were put back on, it became popular to run brakes. We're talking about the style changing over eight years. Now, everybody's ready for the motorcycle they tore apart 20 years ago.'

Bang was well aware of the prejudice suffered by bikers and the way they were lumped together as bad guys: 'Bikers are like the old cowboys. Remember the old days? The cowboys would come galloping into town and they were rough and ready guys.

And some of those guys were real honest. Real Honest, think about that. Some of them wouldn't take a nickel off a guy if he was passed out drunk. But they'd come rolling into town and they loved to drink and yell and chase women. They had good fun – rollicking jolly good fun. Those guys became obsolete. They'd come to town and have too much fun, they'd scare the shit out of the straight people. We ain't no different from the cowboys – they did it a hundred years ago. The girls would be in the saloons just like they are today.'

There were problems at Daytona and Sturgis in the early eighties when the freewheeling chopper lifestyle repeatedly brought the scooter tramps into conflict with

OPPOSITE and THIS PAGE
A chopped Shovelhead built by Bill in Bristol, England. It is based around a custom, rigid frame, a stock Harley gas tank, apehangers and a custom rear fender and features a jockey shift. The painted scallop design is reminiscent of the hot-rod era.

Two eighties approaches to building a Knucklehead in a custom rigid frame: stock rear fender and tank with custom seat and drum brake telescopic front end (opposite) and bobbed rear fender, Mustang tank and short twin-disc front end (left).

authority. To the tramps who frequented the scene, it all seemed trivial enough, drinking on the street, public nudity, no rear-view mirror, apehangers too high, exhaust pipes too loud – all leading to fines and nights in jail. Despite this, the chopper guys refused to go away, they were determined to stay. 'When was the last time you saw a beatnik? Or better yet, a hippie? Where are the people who screamed "freedom" in the '60s and

'70s? Outlaw bikers were an important part of the culture of the '60s and '70s. And now in the '80s, out of all the craziness of the last 20 years, only the [motorcycle] brotherhood has survived,' wrote Peter Boyles in *Denver Magazine* during 1982.

While he was asking a valid question in the light of drastically changing times, it also illustrated the strength of the biker scene. In a little over 30 years it had become a solid

and constant part of the general run of things. As AMF's market share declined, only this one large group of riders – the hard-core bikers – remained faithful to Harley-Davidson products, and when the fad for Japanese-powered choppers had passed away and the fickle had switched to other pastimes, these were the ones who kept the concept of the chopper, and indeed the Harley rider, alive, even though, in the manner of popular

RIGHT
Chopped Duo Glide-type Panhead with
overstock forks, apehangers and bobbed
rear fender.

OPPOSITE
Chopped Knucklehead with long
springers, apehangers and flame paint
job.

ABOVE
Styles evolve slowly and seventies-style choppers were gradually refined into eighties types and so on.

RIGHT and OPPOSITE
Clive Maye's chopped Panhead. This Panhead is based around a straightleg frame but uses a later telescopic raked-out front end along with a custom seat and neatly fabricated rear fender struts.

outlaws, they maintained a defiant attitude to society in general.

Here is a sample of the biker's philosophy of life from J.F. Freedman's novel, *Against the Wind*: 'Some of the boys mosey over and start talking bikes [which means Harleys, of course], Panheads and Knuckles and suicide shifters and if you never rode an old Indian, man, you don't know what it is to get your kidneys scrambled permanent, and then some of the ladies start hovering [all the world knows ladies love outlaws] ... straight society can't handle the truth they [bikers] lay on the world so they've got to cut them down, categorize them, call them outlaws. Anyway so what if they are outlaws, that's the American way ...'

The novel is about members of the Scorpions MC but their attitude to life goes far beyond a single club or novel. It goes on, 'F*** riceburners, f*** all foreign bikes: a real biker, and most definitely any outlaw biker, whatever colors he wears, rides a Harley. It's part of the unwritten law; you buy American and you ride American. No draft-dodging pussies here, either'.

True American bikers rode Harleys, union-made on American soil, and were proud patriots into the bargain. They didn't start that crazy Asian war but had proudly stood and faced Charlie behind an M16 and Old Glory at Khe Sahn and all the other hellholes, because freedom isn't free. The bewilderment of a working man (bikers are predominantly working-class) seeing his class and kin unemployed while the country was squandering dollars on ever-increasing numbers of imports spawned the bumper stickers and T-shirts that read, 'Hungry? Out of work? Eat your riceburner', and 'Buy American – the job you save might be your own'.

Bikers regarded these as laudable sentiments but remained alienated from the mainstream of American society all the same, shunned, ironically, by the country of which they were so proud. Perceived as crude, rude and unrefined they were regarded as beyond the pale by many and were frequently treated as second-class citizens. Such treatment came in many forms, from refused service in bars

and restaurants while on the road, subjection to more than their fair share of attention from traffic cops, having club runs stopped at roadblocks and their constitutional rights infringed. Hard-core bikers saw it as the price they had to pay for living differently, and sought consolation in the fact that they were having more fun than most.

Led by Vaughn Beals, who had joined Harley-Davidson in 1975 as vice-president, a group of 13 Harley-Davidson executives raised $100 million and bought the company from AMF in 1981, leading to the evocative advertising phrase, 'The eagle soars alone'. In April 1982, *Easyriders* magazine reported that 'Harley currently sells only 31% of bikes

OPPOSITE
Poetry in motion: a straightleg-framed Panhead chopper.

LEFT and ABOVE
A rigid-framed Shovelhead chopper at Red River in New Mexico and (above) another variation on the theme in the form of Keith Chadburn's bike, seen at Daytona Bikeweek.

OPPOSITE and LEFT
This rigid Shovelhead is constructed
from custom parts in the area around its
engine, transmission and fatbob gas
tank. It has a rear disc brake, no front
brake, magneto ignition and uses a
custom seat mounted on a minimal rear
fender.

soon encountered stormy skies. Between 1980 and 1982 Harley-Davidson had to lay off a portion of its workforce and the management appealed to the government to increase tariffs on imported Japanese motorcycles of over 43-ci (700-cc) displacement.

Harley-Davidson perceived the heavyweights coming in from Japan, such as the Honda Goldwing, as its main threat. Consequently, the U.S. Government, under the presidency of Ronald Reagan, decided to impose tariffs of up to 50 per cent on such imports and Reagan himself went as far as to visit one of Harley-Davidson's plants.

Better days were around the corner for the company, however, and in 1983 another new engine was announced, officially designated the Evolution. This was to be Harley-Davidson's salvation and by 1984 motorcycle magazines were able to report that its laid-off workers had now been re-employed, its market share had increased and that the company had made a profit for the first time in three years.

Vaughn Beals of Harley-Davidson was quoted as saying: 'We're not out of the woods yet but we're working hard to get there. We have an obligation to the American people and the government to take advantage of the breathing room the tariffs provide. We intend to fulfil that obligation by finishing up the job at hand.' One of the ways the company achieved this is by aggressively marketing the new engine, whose name, Evolution, was entirely appropriate: the bottom end of the 80-ci (1311-cc) engine could trace its origins back

in the over 1000cc market. Honda has a 26% share, Kawasaki has 16% and the other Japanese manufacturers are coming on like Yamamoto at Pearl Harbor'. Vaughn Beals, asked why AMF was abandoning Harley-Davidson, was quoted as saying, 'Aggression is the key word in this industry, without it you lose your market and AMF had lost the will to fight for Harley-Davidson's share of the market.'

According to Beals, AMF had spent vast sums on plant-building and modernization after buying Harley-Davidson and had decided not to pump in any more. 'It had to justify Harley-Davidson's expenses against those of its 30 or 40 other businesses,' Beals recalled, 'but those of us who were running AMF's motorcycle products group had to justify what was right for Harley against what was right for AMF. It was a stand-off. AMF considered our offer as a sort of last resort.' Soar alone though the eagle did, it

RIGHT
An eighties incarnation of the rigid-framed chopper: custom rigid frame, twin disc front end, single disc rear and alternator Shovelhead engine.

OPPOSITE
Bill Bultz of Omaha, Nebraska on his chopped 1975 FX.

through the Shovelhead and Panhead to the original 61E Knucklehead of 1936. It was the one major factor that saved Harley-Davidson from going out of business and re-established it as a major force among the ranks of the world's motorcycle producers.

Peter C. Reid, writing in a business study of Harley-Davidson's renaissance entitled, *Well Made in America*, discusses Harley's customer base before its remarkable change of fortune. He writes, without a trace of irony, 'These Harley riders run. About half are supervisors, machine operators and other skilled workers. But Harley riders also include lawyers, doctors, bankers, entertainers, engineers, and scientists. Perhaps 1 per cent belong to the Hell's Angels end of the spectrum.' Exactly.

While the Milwaukee factory was perfecting its Evolution engine, chopper-building continued in the garages and backyards of bikers around the world. The dominant style was still the various permutations of the FX Super Glide. The major components were still rigid and there were swing-arm frames, telescopic and spring front ends and Panhead and

Shovelhead motors. The process of chopper building is not without its difficulties, a fact noted by Daniel Wolf in his book, *The Rebels, a Brotherhood of Outlaw Bikers*: 'Chopping is the last stage and the ultimate challenge in personalizing a motorcycle. The biker not only rebuilds the entire machine; he virtually redesigns it. When a biker spends a couple of thousand dollars on a used Harley FLH at a police auction with the intention of doing a "chop job" he has bought into his share of the hassles, grief and broken knuckles and the frustration of hours of hard work and inevitable mistakes.' He goes on to say: 'The practical side of chopping is that it allows a biker to turn a used and inexpensive rat bike [poor condition] into a symbol of power and status.'

During the mid-eighties the fashion for rideable street choppers continued to involve rigid and swing-arm frames and both springer and telescopic front ends, although increasingly newer components were used and cast-alloy wheels, supplied by Harley as original equipment, appeared in greater numbers, as did disc brakes simply because many of the second-hand Harleys that were chopped had these items as stock. The aftermarket custom parts industry also adapted its products to suit the evolving motorcycles, and fatbob fenders for FXR frames, strutless rear fenders and low sissy bars for strutless fenders all made an appearance.

The long, low bikes that had become popular in the San Francisco Bay Area in the early seventies were still being constructed, although by the mid-eighties the style had

reached its peak. This style had been developed by Arlen Ness, Ron Simms and others in California and had become popular all over the U.S.A., but by this time, bikers were looking for more rideable styles. Bill Gardner of GMA in Omaha, Nebraska, was quoted as saying about just such a bike he had recently built, 'I hate to say it, but I think

it's really kind of dead now. More people are into rideability these days. They want a bike they can get on and ride anywhere. These are really just bar-to-bar bikes. You can't ride them seriously.'

Arlen Ness built one of the most radical of these machines in 1985, based around an FX Super Glide engine and transmission,

OPPOSITE and ABOVE
This FX chopper is based around the standard frame that has been extensively modified. Its twin disc brake front end and solid rear wheel give the bike a performance image, though the minimal rear fender and Sportster tank are traditional chopper features.

RIGHT and OPPOSITE
Tig Leake from Leesburg, Florida, built
this classic rigid chop by combining a
1957 straightleg big-twin frame and a
1974 big-twin engine.

although these were modified extensively and the engine was equipped with a Magnuson Supercharger, while the frame and most of the other components were custom-made especially for the project. By this time, the style of low riders had strayed so far from choppers that while these machines were undoubtedly custom bikes they were no longer choppers from the 'high bars and rigid

frames' school of thought. Ness went on to take the style to new extremes when he built an even more radical scooter with similar lines in its design, the bike being based around a 128-ci (2097-cc) V-twin engine. The Bay Area styling in a less extreme form was popular and Harley's FXLR of 1986 was a testament to this, its LR suffix designating the bike Low Rider. It featured a rubber-

mounted Evolution engine as well as a 21-in (53-cm) laced front wheel and a 16-in (41-cm) solid rear.

The marketing of the Evolution Harleys, the founding of the Harley Owners Group (HOG) – seen by some as an attempt by Harley-Davidson to reclaim motorcycling's family tradition – and the increasing numbers of a new generation of 'celebrities' now

ABOVE
Different influences altered the
appearances of some choppers in the
mid-eighties: this is a 1980 FX low rider
built by Arlen Ness that clearly takes a
lot of its style from the drag strip.

OPPOSITE
A classy, rideable alternator-Shovelhead
chopper that comprises just the right
combination of factory and custom
Harley-Davidson parts.

riding Harleys, all combined to make Harley-Davidson ownership more than simply desirable; all of a sudden it was the hottest fashion accessory anyone could have.

Meanwhile, those who had stuck with Harley through thick and thin were somewhat bemused by the turnaround in fashion. They were shocked to see that, having been shunned by the establishment for so long, their reason for living was suddenly a fashion statement. They did not dig the pre-ripped jeans and designer T-shirts

and were surprised when posh nightspots suddenly welcomed 'bikers'. They had been raised on choppers – flatheads, Knuckles and Pans. For many, this was way before even the Shovelheads – though they undoubtedly made great chops too – so they didn't need some damn yuppie telling them what was cool.

Not for nothing did a new rash of stickers suddenly appear, 'If motorcycling was a family thing Harleys would have four doors' and the considerably more blunt, 'Die

Yuppie Scum'. It was a similar story for the Vietnam Veterans: sick of being vilified for their involvement in the war they formed a club, with one obvious requirement for membership. They flew a patch that left no one in any doubt about who they were or where they had been. Pressure brought to bear by them and others, with events such as the run to the Wall – the Vietnam War Memorial in Washington – helped to bring POW/MIA issues to the fore.

As the eighties drew to a close, choppers

were still running on the streets and even if some of the prominent builders and shops were concentrating on building low riders and modifying Evos, the guys at home were still there with a rigid frame up on a beer crate, a pile of parts and the determination to see the job through. Daniel Wolf noted that, 'Many of the decisions a biker makes while chopping his hog will reflect a solidifying of his outlaw-biker attitude, especially if his choices fly in the face of what the motorcycle industry would consider standard

OPPOSITE
The almost timeless classic Shovelhead chopper: springers, flames, chain and rigid frame.

LEFT
This chopped down big twin uses a clever mixture of stock Harley parts, as well as some modified ones, and a few custom parts to create the classic chopper shape.

RIGHT and OPPOSITE
A Shovelhead chop with a Sportster tank,
mounted Frisco-style, on the frame's top
tube. Springer forks, straight pipes and a
bobbed rear fender accentuate the
radical appearance.

safety features and technological
advancements, and what outsiders consider
common sense features. For example, he will
have to choose between having a springer
front end that uses an antiquated system of
cushioning the ride with external springs, and
a "glide" front end with hydraulic shock
absorbers that has been used in modern
production motorcycles since 1949 [in the
U.S.A., earlier elsewhere]. If the biker
chooses the brute strength and "boss looks"
of the sculptured steel springer over the
comfortable-riding but plain-looking glide
front end, he makes a strong statement within
the outlaw community. Along with the choice
of forks goes the choice of frames. A biker
who runs with a springer front end will also
likely choose the smooth classic lines of a
rigid frame – affectionately referred to as a
"hardtail" – that has no rear shock absorbers,
as opposed to a juice frame that compromises
bone-clean looks for the comfort of rear
shocks. Fellow bikers again will appreciate
the sacrifice that this choice entails: "Hard
tails are for hard asses".' With a rare flash of
inspiration in his otherwise rancorous book,
Yves Lavigne sums it up even more
succinctly: 'A chopper, although it looks
sleek and graceful, is a bitch of a machine to
handle.' Who cares so long as it's a class act?

CHAPTER FIVE
THE NINETIES:
THE HIGH-TECH ERA

The decade began on a high note as the two biggest biker bashes of the year, Daytona and Sturgis, celebrated their 50th anniversaries and drew record crowds to Florida and South Dakota. Just when it was safe to think that everything that could be done with choppers had already been done, something altogether new arrived on the scene.

As the nineties began, the Evolution engine was proving popular and was being used in the construction of traditional rigid-framed choppers, while the so-called master-builders of the Hamsters MC and others were still concentrating on long, low machines that combined elements of styling from Bay Area Low Riders and the quarter-mile drag-strip machines. The transition from the eighties to the nineties was, like that of previous decades, a gradual one, an indication of which can be seen in the bikes featured in magazines of the time – usually the cream of the crop – which still included machines finished with engraved parts and gold-leaf scrolled paintwork, while springers and rigid frames are also still to be seen.

Meanwhile, on the world stage, the

various allies forming the coalition were deploying their armies into Saudi Arabia in Desert Shield and later Desert Storm, to liberate Kuwait from the Iraqi army which occupied it. The U.S. Army and Air Force were among these forces but, unlike Vietnam, went to war with public opinion solidly behind them, to return to a welcoming reception. Elsewhere, the computer technology that was being used to direct

lathes and milling machines was the catalyst for change within custom-bike building, because it enabled the widespread use of billet aluminium for the manufacture of a new range of custom components.

All of a sudden, there were replacement billet parts for almost every part of a motorcycle. Brake and clutch master cylinders, brake calipers, engine and transmission dress-up items, fender struts,

wheels, twistgrips and more. One of the first of the major exponents of billet parts was Arlen Ness, who was also one of the builders who brought old-style choppers back to the forefront of custom biking. He built a rigid-framed Knucklehead chop that was old-style in shape and silhouette but up-to-the-minute in detail, with components such as disc brakes and a number of billet-alloy parts, such as forward controls and master

OPPOSITE
Flamboyant decoration and high-tech components typified the nineties, all of which can be seen in this rigid Panhead, with its purple and yellow paint job and high-performance brake discs and calipers.

BELOW LEFT
A basic but classy nineties chopper built by Kes of the Outlaws MC, England.

PAGE 152
This is a long Swedish-style chopper base built around an Evolution big-twin engine.

PAGE 153
Even traditionally styled choppers benefited from the high-tech components, using massive numbers of spokes in laced wheels and billet-aluminium in the form of the air cleaner cover seen on this bike.

cylinders. Alongside the steadily increasing use of billet-aluminium on the low rider style of custom bike, the rigid-framed chop was also being slowly refined. While Evolution engines and alloy wheels had become commonplace there were still plenty of choppers appearing with Sportster tanks. Increasing numbers of fatbobs were appearing – rigid and swing-arm framed Harley chops with the large-capacity old-style Harley gas tank. This coincided with the massive boom in popularity of Harley-Davidson motorcycles worldwide.

The factory increased its production considerably and exported more motorcycles to more countries than ever before. This

OPPOSITE
Logie's rigid chopper is powered by an Evolution big twin. Its styling relies on a combination of modern and traditional parts.

LEFT
Steve Mastine's traditional-style swing-arm Shovelhead chopper has a paint job typical of the nineties.

BELOW LEFT
A pared-to-the-bone rigid chopper powered by an Evolution big-twin engine. A neat detail is the profile of cut flames on the axle adjusters at the rear of the frame.

155

massive boom in demand had several effects:
it increased the demand for accessories and
custom parts and enabled the aftermarket
industry based on custom Harley parts to
flourish and achieve considerable expansion.
Manufacturers producing billet-alloy parts
multiplied, as did those offering components
such as custom fenders and handlebars.

Two types were manufactured during this
boom, bolt-on parts and the components to
construct complete bikes in the chopper
tradition if not the style. The bolt-ons were
designed for the owners of stock new
Harleys seeking to modify their motorcycles
without completely reconstructing them.

An example can be seen in the 1992
Custom Chrome catalogue: Part No. 13-204.
Fat Bob Rear Fender Kit for FXR models.
This was '... for all FXR models from 1982
through 1986 and 1987 through 1991 FXRTs.
The rebellious upswept kick of the chopper-
style rear fender is combined with our
smooth, chromed steel fender struts that not
only improve styling but provide improved
fender support over the original equipment
parts. Accepts all of CCI's tail light kits with
Fat Bob mounts, or the stock (OEM 59993-
80) tail light bracket. This kit and its
components are not compatible with Original
Equipment or aftermarket sissy bars.'

This description leaves no doubt as to
which stock Harleys the kit is intended.
Another set of parts was available to do the
same job on other models, such as 13-206 for
FXST, FXSTC and FXSTS models from
1984 through 1991. In some ways bolt-on
parts such as these are the antithesis of the
chopper philosophy, simply because the

chopper builder will cut and shut something to fit. As a result Custom Chrome part No. 13-178, a Custom Fat Bob Rear Fender would be more suited to their bikes, as it came without holes or tail light bracket, leaving the purchaser to drill them to suit his needs. The fact that a fatbob rear fender is included in a large parts catalogue at all is of

interest and illustrates how established certain fashions had become within the world of chopped Harleys.

The fatbob fender came about when early builders used a front fender on the rear of their bikes in place of the original hinged one. The stock front fender on a Harley with springer forks featured a turned-out rear lip

which, when fitted over the rear wheel with the rear edge approximately a quarter rotation up from its original position, had the effect of turning up the rear lip of the now rear fender. In the old days this was a straightforward operation because chances were that the bike, about to become a bobber, had had one fitted when it was purchased. As

A high-tech nineties version of bobber styling. Its rigid frame, wide bars and black with flames paintwork sit comfortably with the high-performance front end and spoked alloy wheels.

the decades passed, springer fenders have become scarcer, so the aftermarket industry produced bobbed rear fenders pressed with a cutaway for the drive chain already in place and the advantage of no holes whatsoever, unlike a cut-down stock fender.

Like other parts manufacturers mentioned in this book, Custom Chrome Inc. was established in the early decades of chopper building and, as well as the new range of bolt-on parts described above, offer components that appeal to chopper builders

such as a rigid frame – Part No. 08-914 – for big twins with a neck rake increased by 3 to 33° and 2in (5cm) extra in the front frame downtubes to accommodate this alteration. This was one of several variations on nine different frames listed in 1992. That

catalogue also listed the service parts fundamental to keeping a Harley, either stock or chopped, on the road, including gasket sets, brake pads and tyres. In the same year, Minnesota-based Drag Specialties produced a similarly large annual catalogue but

concentrated more on service parts and accessories. It didn't, for example, list complete frames.

Those who advertised as manufacturers and distributors of custom parts in the early nineties showed a marked increase over those

of earlier decades and included Sumax, Drag Specialties, Forking by Frank, Antique Cycle Supply, Nempco Inc., Andrews Products Inc., HOG Hollow, Hippy's M/C Parts, KüryAkyn, LBV Engineering, David Sarafan Inc., J&P Cycles, Performance Machine Inc.,

People still built traditional choppers in the nineties. This rigid Panhead is timeless apart from the paint job, which indicates the era in which the bike was built.

OPPOSITE and LEFT
During the nineties Arlen Ness built a
number of choppers that cleverly
combined old-school styling cues with
modern billet components from his own
range of aftermarket products. The
Shovelhead- and Evolution-powered
bikes have flame paint jobs on their
extensive taildragger fenders, while all
three feature rigid frames, apehangers
and springers.

PAGE 164
This nineties Ness chopper uses
traditional components such as the
Shovelhead engine, rigid frame and
springer forks, but has many high-tech
billet-aluminium components. Note the
flames machined into the air cleaner
cover insert and the grips. Also made
from billet are the front brake master
cylinder and tail-light mount.

PAGE 165
This Ness chopper takes the mixture of
old and new components further, in that
performance brake components are
combined with springer forks and the
traditional hot-rod flame paint job is
completed in modern colours.

Mike Corbin, Arlen Ness, Cycle Supply, Superior Motorcycle Parts and Accessories, Tripoli MFG, White Bros., Mustang, Barnett, Cycle Shack, Chrome Specialties, Delkron, James Gaskets, Jay Brake, Manley, Morris, Paughco, Primo, Rivera, Rowe, S&S, STD, Lightning Cycle Parts, Dragon Precision Machining, Nostalgia Cycle, Graves Plating, Custom Chrome Inc., Samson and Mid-U.S.A. Cycle Parts Inc. The scale of the growing aftermarket parts industry and its phenomenal growth in that period meant that it was possible eventually to build a complete motorcycle that looked like a Harley-Davidson but used no genuine parts whatsoever. Later companies supplying complete 'American' motorcycles would also appear, with names including Mirage, Illusion, Big Dog, Titan and more. Many of these followed the contemporary style established by the factory's big twins but offered more potent engine packages and custom paintwork.

The factory was also heavily into

followed by the FXSTSB Bad Boy, possibly the one most approximating a Hollister-era bobber that it was possible to make in the last decade of the 20th century, in that factories were hampered by laws regulating turn signals, noise, emissions and lights.

Such machines failed to meet with universal approval: Snow and Sager writing in *Iron Horse* magazine in December 1994 remarked: 'Milwaukee continues to market its approximation of the outlaw aesthetic to consumers as "genuine" when it's no more authentic than a cereal box reproduction of the Great Masters' works. Only the individual can transform his bike into a real custom.' They went on to say of the nineties: 'The success of the factory's stunted redefinition of customization can be seen

nostalgia: the springer fork front end had been reintroduced in 1988 for the company's 85th anniversary and in conjunction with the softail frame looked like an old-time rigid but with the advantage of rear suspension, Harley's new bikes closely resembled those of earlier decades. By the nineties, the style was unmistakably retro and the bikes looked like Hydra Glides and springer Pans, while the Wide Glides and Super Glides looked like older choppers and words like Heritage and Nostalgia began to appear in model names.

The Fat Boy caused something of a furore, looking as it did like no other factory-built motorcycle and with a name that was an amalgam of two bombs dropped on Japan, Fat Man and Little Boy. Like the T-shirt said, 'Two bombs weren't enough'. This was

everywhere, from so-called custom bike shows to the highways to the majority of Harley magazines on the stands.' *Iron Horse* may have had a mixed history itself, but it was always honest about choppers and loyal to the bikers who built and rode them in the nineties.

Now that the factory was putting springers on its production Harleys, it was inevitable that springer-forked choppers should enjoy an upsurge in popularity, and especially the new style of custom Harley, the 'luxury liner'. In other words, these bikes

OPPOSITE
Loud and proud – what it's all about!

LEFT and ABOVE
Jeff Lorimer's nineties version of a swing-arm Panhead chopper. It features a disc rear brake and a strutless rear fender.

RIGHT
A tough modern Evo rigid, built by a
member of the Outlaws MC, Wales.

OPPOSITE
A member of the Hell's Angels MC, New
York City, on his classic generator
Shovelhead chopper. It has a selection of
custom parts and a mixture of factory
Harley parts chosen to give just the right
lines to the overall bike.

were out-garbaging the garbage wagons in
that they featured more bodywork than a
stock factory dresser and were as far
removed from a bare-bones chopper as it was
possible to get without fitting four wheels.
The trend also sparked equal and opposite
reactions which, once again had seen the
dramatic increase in popularity of long-
forked choppers. A major exponent of the
revived style, but with a new twist, was Pat
Kennedy, who runs a shop in Tombstone,
Arizona. He had seen the particular style of
choppers built in Sweden, with enormously
long telescopic front ends, and had built
choppers in that style in the U.S.A.

It seemed that anything went in the
nineties, and low riders, high-performance
Harleys, dressers, luxury liners, garbage
wagons, choppers, nostalgia choppers and
billet-adorned stockers were all to be seen.
What they all had in common, apart from V-
twin power plants, was that they utilized
high-tech components and techniques with,
for example, Mig and Tig welding helping to
advance building techniques. The truth is that
though fashions go in circles and this is as
true of chopper building as anything else, the
custom market of the late nineties was
returning to the idea of change for change's
sake, which often results in ostentatious,
overweight bikes as well as bikes that bear
no resemblance to the basic brutal chopper.

One of the reasons for this was due to
the increasing numbers which now regarded
a Harley as a fashion accessory, which was
very different from the attitude of ordinary
scooter trash. The latter frequently wore T-
shirts that read, 'It's not about riding

motorcycles anymore. It's a f****** fashion show', which is confirmed in *Outlaw Machine*, where Brock Yates makes this insightful comment: 'Tamer bikers who have arrived in recent years have significantly diminished the Sturgis street action. It has become more a massive fashion show than a legitimate biker conclave. For every One Percenter in Sturgis there are a hundred poseurs vamping up and down Main Street on their $30,000 Arlen-Ness-inspired customs, towing their incredible blonde ladies in show-me-some-tits leather and glue-on tattoos. They shamelessly imitate the outlaw bikers.' It is the same at Daytona,

OPPOSITE
Many of the bikes belonging to Hell's Angels feature painstakingly airbrushed winged death's heads in the club's colours on the sides of the gas tanks. These are good examples from the Hell's Angels MC, New York.

LEFT and ABOVE
Rack 'em Up is a traditionally-styled but nineties-built rigid chopper. It features modern parts such as an Evolution engine and was built by Chrome Specialties Inc.

RIGHT
A fifties-inspired though nineties-built version of a bobber, built around a Shovelhead engine.

OPPOSITE
Steve Green's bare-boned rigid Evolution chopper. It seems that flames never go out of style.

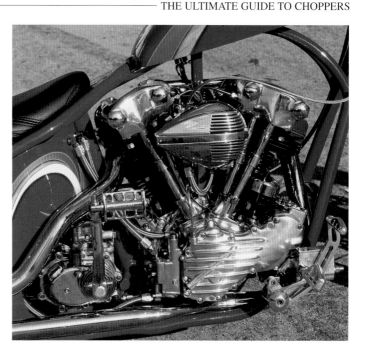

where in 2004 a One Percenter was photographed in a T-shirt that read 'Years ago you wanted to kill us, now you want to be one of us.' Ain't it the truth?

Sturgis in the nineties can be summed up in terms of Chrome, Silicone and Testosterone. Johnson's Corner is a gas station truckstop and on the first weekend of Sturgis the waitresses were wearing black Harley T-shirts. One might ask what's so special about that? except that Johnson's Corner is approximately 400 miles (640km) from Sturgis. The Colorado truckstop is on

OPPOSITE
A traditional type of chopper with apehangers and upswept fishtail exhausts, built entirely with new parts during the nineties. The engine is an Evolution fitted with Xzotic covers that give the appearance of a Panhead.

LEFT and ABOVE
Milwaukee Iron of Lynchburg, Virginia, unveiled this retro-chopper in Daytona in 1997. It is powered by a Knucklehead engine.

OPPOSITE and THIS PAGE
While the Milwaukee Iron chopper is a
modern interpretation of the sixties
choppers, the Evolution chopper of Ian
Borrowman (seen with his bike) is a
modern interpretation of the popular and
extreme Swedish style.

I-25 north from Denver and a popular stop for those headed north to the rally, so for a couple of weeks a year the normal crowd of customers, truckers, cowboys and tourists are outnumbered by Harley aficionados headed for South Dakota.

As bikes are refuelled, there is the endless spectacle of Harleys ripping past against the backdrop of the front range of the Rocky Mountains, which surely must be one of motorcycling's most spectacular scenes. The next town on this route to Sturgis is Lusk where, in a bar called the Silver Dollar, the cowboys spend their time ogling the biker women and, in their own words, 'getting bowlegged', which brings to mind Quinn's toast in _Jaws_, 'Here's to swimmin'

with bowlegged women'. It is said that cowboys have three pairs of jeans: one the right size for the rodeo, a size too big for practising for the rodeo and a size too small for the dance afterwards. Across the street is another bar called the Pub, with a sign behind the bar that reads, 'Men, No shirt, no service. Women, No shirt, free drinks!'

Down on Main Street in Sturgis there are a lot of bars and in one, the Dungeon, is Li'l John from Joliet, Illinois, who lives down the road from the Blues Brothers' prison. He'd ridden out the 600 or 700 miles to Sturgis on his 1974 Shovelhead and had to get the tank welded en route. Of his bike he says, 'I built this son of a bitch and I'm keeping it,' and 'the only way to bury an Evo is with a

RIGHT
Pat Kennedy of Tombstone, Arizona, was
a well-known proponent of long-forked
choppers in the nineties. He built these
two for himself and his wife Brooke.

OPPOSITE
Fat back tyre, long telescopic forks, rigid
frame, Sportster tank – all contribute to
this nineties take on the classic rigid
chopper and a cool bike.

Shovel.' The trailering of bikes out to Sturgis was something Li'l John felt strongly about: 'There's one thing worse than a bagger on a trailer. It's two.'

In the sci-fi movie, *Close Encounters*, much of the story centres on an unusual geographical feature. This is known as Devil's Tower and is a place of legend to the Native Americans, who tell how the earth rose up to meet the sky to save some little girls from a predatory bear. In reality, the tower was formed by a plug of lava that was forced through a fissure in the earth's crust, but the legend is more picturesque. We rolled past Devil's Tower – America's first national monument – on the Wednesday of bike week, en route for a tiny place called Hulett. Hulett is in Wyoming rather than South Dakota, which means the laws are different and less zealously enforced. There are only two cops in Hulett, so reinforcements from local counties are drafted in to help out. As a result, the town hosts a biker day which the old hands regard as more like the wilder days of Sturgis, with beer-drinking in the streets and a general party atmosphere. Given the amount of female flesh on view, it was amusing to see Leo Zawilla from Illinois selling disposable cameras from his bagger for ten bucks, which showed considerable enterprise, especially as they were selling like the proverbial hot cakes! The event was well worth the trip out from Sturgis.

Another popular destination in the other direction is Mount Rushmore, where the faces of four U.S. presidents, Washington, Jefferson, Lincoln and Roosevelt can be seen carved into the cliff face. Spearfish is another small town outside Sturgis and written on the bathroom wall in a bar called the Back Porch is a slogan that reads, 'If you're too scared to ride the muthafucker here give it to your sister'.

There's something of a biker backlash against trailering a Harley. Bellied up to the bar here was an extrovert called Lee from Phoenix and a couple from Denver who were the proud owners of one of the last Shovels, a 1984 Wide Glide. While talking to them, I was reminded of some of the magazines that describe American Harley events as full of 'iguana-heads', people who walk down Main Street with some such animal on their heads. The truth is that there are plenty more real bikers with interesting tales to tell than these but, sadly, many photographers only ever point a lens at the iguana-heads or the granny in the body web, or the fool who has built a motorized armchair. It's far more interesting to talk to the guy who's been riding for 20 years or more and is still rightly and genuinely proud of his Shovelhead.

There are campsites all around Sturgis, and these are like little bike weeks and biker parties in miniature, with some of them, like the Buffalo Chip and the Glencoe legends in their own right. Another is Hog Heaven, where there are numerous custom bike producers offering for sale what look like custom Harleys straight out of the box, including Ultra, Big Dog, Extreme Cycle

OPPOSITE
A classy combination of old and new. Springer forks and a rigid frame are combined with an Evolution engine and disc brakes and finished off with flames.

LEFT
Charlie behind the bars of his nineties rigid chopper.

RIGHT and OPPOSITE
Charlie's bike, 'Nice 'n' Sleazy,
combines traditional chopper themes
such as flames, apehangers and a rigid
frame with numerous high-tech
processes, including performance tyres
and brakes, many-spoked wheels and
billet- aluminium components.

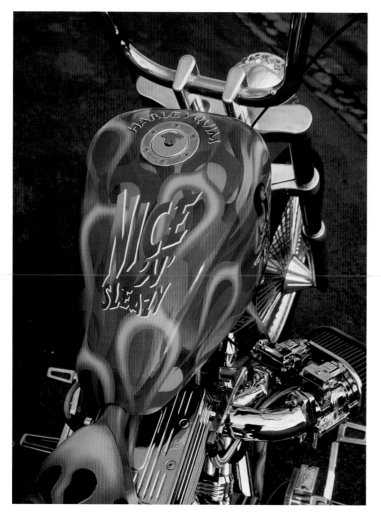

Works, Panzer. Then there are the California Motor Company Indians, powered by engines that owe more in design to Harley-D. Add to this the new American cruisers such as Polaris, and not forgetting the Jap manufacturers and the more obscure, such as the Enfield India, and it can be seen that motorcycling is alive and well in the U.S.A.

In a house with a crowd of bikers from Texas was a retired guy who used to own an Indian dealership and had been out at Sturgis back in 1940. He'd known Pappy Hoel, who founded the rally, and liked to regale us with tales of racing back then, for example, one of a guy with a Rudge who used an Indian piston, fitted to the bike and tested right outside the shop, to keep his bike in contention. There isn't room for all the stories here, but here's one for the engineers to ponder: to increase the oiling capability of the old flatheads they used to knurl the piston skirts so that they would drag more oil up the bores!

The Jackpine Gypsies was the club that founded the event before the Second World War and is still in business. It hosts the short-track dirt-track racing, the hill climb and the Gypsy Tour around which it was originally all based. Some of America's big four patch clubs come to Sturgis each year and this particular year was no exception. I happened to be walking down the street behind some Texas Bandidos when they passed some Hell's Angels. To say it resembled a stand-off in a Western movie is probably overstating the case but neither group as much as raised an eyebrow in the other's direction. Others flying their patches in Sturgis were members

of the Sturgis Police Department; these came in fours, and with pistols on their hips regularly patrolled the bars, such as Gunner's Lounge, where the One Percenter clubs were drinking. Again, it was impossible to avoid making comparisons with cowboy movies of the past.

The media and law enforcement agencies remain fascinated by the One Percenters and major clubs like the Bandidos, Breed, Hell's Angels and the Outlaws, Pagans and Sons of Silence face continual scrutiny. Despite almost half a century of chopper history having elapsed, as recently as 1994 the best definition of a chopper that the Royal Canadian Mounted Police could come up with, in an investigation into outlaw motorcycle clubs, was the following flawed description: 'Chopper: chopped or cut down motorcycle. All unnecessary equipment is stripped off the bike including the front brake and fenders. The wheel fork is extended and the handlebars are set high.' There is an irony in this because the type of chopper ridden by the One Percenter of the nineties had evolved from the basic chopper of yore. Nowadays, it tends to be much closer to stock but modified in a specific way that means a significant number of outlaw club bikes can be identified at a glance.

This more practical style reflects both the need for mobility and the distances to be covered. DJ Andy Kershaw, interviewing Sonny Barger for *The Observer* magazine of 19 September 1993, touched on this when he wrote, 'Choppers, it seems, are a thing of the past. When he [Barger] hits that highway to hell he does so, at a steady 55mph, on a

OPPOSITE and LEFT
Rudy, of the Hell's Angels MC, Frisco, and one of the proprietors of California Choppers, built this FXR-based chopper around a custom FXR frame, a 100-ci (1639-cc) S&S Evolution engine and a performance front end, wheels and brakes.

RIGHT and OPPOSITE
Caz's bike. John Carroll wanted an old-style, jockey-shift flathead chopper that had a few modern touches. This was the result, a 1942 WLC engine in a custom rigid frame with a Sportster tank, apehangers and a few billet-aluminium parts such as a Ness brake master cylinder and grips.

standard Harley-Davidson FXRT, a sensible middle-of-the-range tourer favoured by sensible middle-aged men.' In spite of this, those in the know would immediately identify Barger's bike as belonging to a Hell's Angel.

By 1995, Chrome Specialties Inc. of Texas, itself only launched in 1984 by the Kuelbs brothers, had acquired Jammer Cycle Products and included the brand in its 760-page catalogue. It was not alone, for Minnesota's Drag Specialties catalogue for 1995 numbered 735 pages, while New York-based Nempco had an 882-page catalogue and that of Custom Chrome Inc. for the same

year had 768 pages. Part No. 08-914 – the Big-Twin Rigid Frame – was still listed, proving that in spite of all the other trends within the Harley riding spectrum the chopper-builder was still alive and well.

Not everyone buys a custom frame, even now, and it's still not uncommon to see choppers based on modified factory frames – be they swing-arm or rigids. While the styles of real choppers vary in detail, the one most often seen is the one based around a rigid or a swing-arm frame, with a long front end and either a fatbob or Sportster tank. Types and diameters of wheels, lengths and rakes of

OPPOSITE and THIS PAGE
Dick Tree built this nineties rigid around an Evolution engine, giving it a fat back tyre and mounting the tank Frisco-style. It features disc-braked wheels, apehangers and nothing that's not essential to make it go.

front ends, type of rear fenders, all vary, as do the type of hubs, brakes, gearshifts, amount of chrome and choice of paint. The latter two finishes vary according to the amount of money the builder has at his disposal, what his bike is about – 'chrome don't get ya home' – and what he is trying to achieve. There are exceptions: for example, softail frames are used in choppers, although some builders don't like them because they are imitation hardtails, i.e. not real.

Keith Ball touches on the continuing motivation to ride choppers: 'Have you ever experienced 100mph plus, blasted between a labyrinth of cars on a congested freeway or heard the unforgettable sound of handcuffs cinching your hands together behind your back? If not, there's no way I can explain the

OPPOSITE
Arlin Fatland built this modern version of an old bike in Denver. It features a custom frame, an old-time drum-braked front wheel, a scalloped paint scheme and a Knucklehead engine.

LEFT
Bugsy built this rigid alternator Shovelhead chopper, placing a selection of popular chopper components into a great-looking silver-and-blue package that epitomizes the triangular shape of many rigid choppers.

exhilaration, the challenge, the fear or the overt frenzy of building and riding a custom motorcycle.' Of choppers themselves, Ball claims that 'torches and a hell-bent for leather attitude built choppers. Tight upper lips, impunity, too much whiskey and fistfights built these long, lean and mean machines. Breaking laws made choppers fast, loose women made 'em shiny and freedom made them last'.

Much to the chagrin of law enforcement agencies, the Hell's Angels Motorcycle Club celebrated its 50th anniversary during 1998. During the nineties it seemed that the greatest future threat to choppers and their riders was not that their numbers would diminish or their creativity desert them, but one of bureaucracy – the possibility of being legislated off the road. Already in some European countries it was illegal to modify a motorcycle, while in others the laws concerning modifications were positively draconian. New laws governing youngsters obtaining licences and riding motorcycles appeared to deter rather than encourage, while the compulsory wearing of helmets was seen as the thin end of the wedge.

The growing popularity of custom motorcycles hadn't always guaranteed an easy road ahead, as revealed by the founder of Excelsior-Henderson Motorcycles, who published a book on the rise and fall of his company. In it he acknowledges that while a person's dream may not always come true, the pursuit of that dream is filled with truths from which other dreamers can profit, which is why Dan Hanlon's book, tracing the rise and fall of Excelsior-Henderson can be

described as instructive. It was selected as a textbook for study by the Graduate School of Business at the University of St. Thomas in Minneapolis.

Riding the American Dream, the official story of Excelsior-Henderson, was published in August 2004, and is Hanlon's account of what worked and what didn't in an eight-year attempt to build the only independent American motorcycle company in 75 years. 'The book chronicles the good, the bad and the ugly,' says Hanlon. 'As an independent proprietary original-equipment motorcycle manufacturer, we had progressed farther than anyone in over a half-century. It wasn't far enough.'

From the years 1993 to 2000, Excelsior-Henderson Motorcycles acquired the rights to the legendary Excelsior and Henderson names, completed an IPO while raising nearly $100 million, and generated revenue of over $30 million by putting $18,000 motorcycles on the road and building a national dealer network. Sadly, it was eventually forced to file for Chapter 11 protection against its creditors.

The plan had been primarily to compete with Harley-Davidson. The two had been rivals in the early 1900s and Hanlon believed they could be again. 'We were using some of the same marketing and branding they were.' In a chapter entitled Road Warriors: How Guerrillas Meet Gorillas, he remarks that Harley-Davidson was the '... gorilla. We had to be guerrillas'. Ultimately, Harley-Davidson managed to persuade independent dealers not to carry Excelsior-Henderson products, a move, he maintains, that made it

unduly difficult to attract and retain dealers. Hanlon was philosophical in that 'A sense of hope, mixed with a focus on reaching specific milestones that would keep us alive to fight another day made us go as far as we did. No matter what happened, we can still dream, and the dream is not over. Dreams never die'.

In 1999, in time for the new century, Harley-Davidson unveiled the latest in its line of air-cooled V-twin engines, the Twin Cam 88. It displaced 88ci (1442cc) and was the company's biggest production so far. It soon found a home in chopper frames, unlike the VRSCA V-Rod engine, released in 2001. This was a liquid-cooled, fuel-injected, overhead-camshaft engine, developed from the VR1000 race bike. The V-Rod was a hit but its complex engine hinted at a sanitized and unmodified future.

CHAPTER SIX
THE 21ST CENTURY: CHOPPERS RULE AGAIN

The 21st century kicked off with a feature in *Easyriders* magazine on the world's first new chopped Excelsior-Henderson and, more importantly, Jesse James' building of a Camel cigarettes promotional bike for R.J. Reynolds in the avant-garde rigid style that would quickly become his trademark. It appeared in the July 2000 issue of *Easyriders* and was one of the most evil-looking choppers to make the cover of the magazine in a long time. It was quickly followed by another new-style, old-style school bike from Chica's Choppers of Huntington Beach, California. In other words, the influential magazine was confirming that choppers were mainstream fashion once again. Denver's Choppers reopened in Nevada after the death of Denver Mullins, the shop's founder three years earlier, and was reopened by his closest friends and associates, including Mondo Porras, who had been with Denver since the earliest days, while choppers were rolling out of shops as diverse as High Country Custom Cycles of Colorado Springs, Colorado Hog Skins Customs of Leesport, Pennsylvania, and Custom Design Studios of Novato, California.

Laconia bike week ran for the 77th time at Weirs Beach in New Hampshire, while the Black Hills Classic in Sturgis, South Dakota, was at its 60th and the more exclusive Redwood Run its 23rd. Questioning the continuing fashion for Harleys, *Easyriders* noted that at Sturgis, and at Daytona earlier in the year, there had been a record numbers of attendees but that the number of 'bikers' was down!

Daytona Bikeweek hit its 60th anniversary in 2001, the same year that the U.S.A. was left in a state of shock after a terrorist attack destroyed the Twin Towers of the World Trade Center in New York. As it came to terms with the magnitude of the attack a new wave of patriotism began to sweep through the country. This manifested itself in many ways and included the building of tribute bikes rather than choppers, of which the most notable was the Orange County Choppers bike.

Hard-core choppers rolled out of shops that included CSI, Martin Brothers, Thundercycle Designs, Easyriders of Dallas, West Coast Choppers, Korn's Cycle, Donnie Smith, Black Swamp Choppers of Ohio and more. Pat Kennedy unveiled another radical, springer-forked bike from his Tombstone, Arizona, shop and Ron Simms of Bay Area Custom Cycles, noted for a style of custom bagger, presented a chopper that was radical. It featured a 24-in (61-cm) overstock telescopic front end, an S&S motor and a Ron Paugh of Paughco swing-arm chopper frame. It was up to the minute but gave a nod to the past with its black with flames hot-rod

paint scheme, while another noted and long-time bike builder, Dave Perewitz, also wheeled out an old-school chopper with 21st-century touches.

As *Easyriders* magazine celebrated its 30th anniversary, proving just how solid the chopper and custom bike movement was, the trend back towards choppers – referred to as 'long bikes' – was gathering momentum; Jesse James was producing the Choppers for

Life rigid Shovelhead, Chica unveiled a 'hot lava' Knucklehead-powered rigid chopper, Paul Yaffe wheeled out 'Snake Eyes', a rigid springer Evo and Denver unveiled a pair of old and new Panhead rigids with springer forks. 'Exiled' Englishman, Russell Mitchell, of Exile Cycles in Sunland, California, again brought matt-black rigids to the fore with his S&S-powered hot rod, while Billy Lane built a Panhead with an Indian front end and they

OPPOSITE and BELOW
Phil Piper of Phil's Chopper Shack built these rigids in different styles. The green Sportster is performance-inspired, while the orange and blue chopper with flames is a modern version of the traditional rigid chopper.

followed thick and fast. 'El Diablo' came out of the West Coast Choppers workshop; Choppers Inc. built some wild rigids, including an old-style hot-rod bobber for parts distributor Chrome Specialties; Paul Yaffe designed a rigid chopper kit bike for custom parts specialist Custom Chrome Inc. of Carlsbad; California-based Custom Cycle Creations built a long, low, springer-equipped

S&S big twin and by July 2003 Easy Riders was able to feature no less than 23 aftermarket custom chopper frames from America's aftermarket industry. This is probably not an exhaustive list but it is indicative of how the latest generation of high-tech choppers was now central to the custom bike scene. Established builders such as Sugar Bear, Billy Lane, Thunder Cycle

Design and Jerry Covington continued to build great choppers and others came to the fore, including Westbury Hot Rods, Kendall Johnson Customs, Young's Choppers, Lucky's Choppers, Twisted Choppers, NYC Customs and Strokers of Dallas.

The fact that choppers had become mainstream was nowhere more obvious than on our TV screens as the media courted the

OPPOSITE

Phil Piper with one of the choppers recently to come out of his shop. It is enormously detailed: the fenders exactly follow the curves of the tyres and the custom frame has clean lines.

BELOW LEFT

Modern engineering techniques have enabled a new style of long bike to be built that incorporates ever more technically advanced components.

new generation of chopper builders that were suddenly far removed from scooter trash. New bikes were media events. The 'Shop Rat Chopper', for example, made its debut at the Woodward Dream Cruise in Michigan and was certainly head-turning. While the one-of-a kind chopper was the first initiative of the Shop Rat Association, the Shop Rat Chopper was a means of introducing itself as a national member-based organization,

designed to re-ignite excitement and pride in America's skilled professionals. The Shop Rat Chopper was built by Orange County Choppers, known to the million viewers of the *American Chopper* programme on the TV Discovery channel. It features a patented rim design, designed and manufactured in Michigan by Chris Salow of the Shop Rat Association, and has a friction drive that sits perpendicularly to the axle, the drive

operating several moving mechanical parts while the wheel turns.

Conceived to turns heads, this chopper was built exclusively by talented mechanics affectionately referred to as 'shop rats', a term describing those who make their living in the skilled trades as well as weekend warriors who use their garages to build choppers. 'Few things are as American as our love of automobiles,' says Shop Rat founder,

Chris Salow. 'These classic icons represent some of the many achievements of our nation's tradesmen and women. We created Shop Rat Association to salute the Americans who really built this country and give them their due. It is especially important now when Americans are seeing jobs going overseas.'

Chris Salow is a life-long enthusiast, devoted to taking apart and rebuilding all manner of things since the age of 12. He has created two successful Michigan-based companies, Salow Machine Works and Metalform. 'I know all my success has been because of the determination, creativity and innovation of my shop rat partners and employees,' says Salow. Celebrating such creativity, Salow created the Shop Rat Association, not only to acknowledge skilled workers but also to empower them through

educational opportunities, technical support, training and competitions. 'We want to change people's perceptions about what it means to work in these trades,' says Salow. 'Young people choosing a profession may not consider that the skilled trades offer them the opportunity to be creative and ingenious and be part of the tradition that made our nation as strong as it is.'

Michigan residents were invited to be first on board with a special introductory offer of membership in the national organization. A key part of the vision of the Shop Rat Association is the Shop Rat Foundation, an independent non-profit-making institution. Created to foster education in the industrial arts, the foundation sponsors high school and career-centred competitions, IT programmes, work-study programmes and internships. It offers

OPPOSITE
ABOVE
A purposeful though, by today's standards, basic chopper.

BELOW LEFT
Long stretched gas tanks have become popular on the new century's choppers.

BELOW RIGHT
One of the wild rides built for the Camel Roadhouse tour.

LEFT
A long-forked bike with a tricky air intake which, although completely contemporary, still has flames on its gas tank.

PAGES 204 and 205
Daytona: riding a chopper is primarily about seeing and being seen.

scholarships, accredited training programmes and company referrals. The programmes challenge young people by teaching them teamwork and creative problem-solving, encouraging innovative thinking, the benchmarks of American industry.

If all that seems a far cry from heavy-duty bikers building choppers from old police Harleys on beer crates in their backyards, consider the recognition given to Jesse James of California's West Coast Choppers. James is also the host of the TV Discovery channel's *Monster Garage*, and appeared at the Welding Show 2003 in Detroit to accept a 'Golden Welding Helmet' award for his role in promoting the image of welding to television viewers worldwide. The helmet was donated by the American Welding Society (AWS) and the show is held at the Cobo Center in downtown Detroit.

Jesse James (recently named one of *People* magazine's 50 sexiest) won the award for the advanced welding technology and creativity used during every episode of the

hit TV series, *Monster Garage*. The American Welding Society is the largest organization in the world dedicated to advancing the science, technology and application of joining materials together, with AWS serving more than 48,500 members in the United States and around the world. AWS let it be known that it was 'proud to honour Jesse and the Discovery channel for their efforts to promote the image of welding to television viewers throughout the world'. The

Discovery channel is one of the United States' two largest cable television networks, delivering informative entertainment to 86.8 million households across the nation.

Choppers received more accolades when the 'Miller Bike' featured in an episode of the Discovery channel's *American Chopper*, celebrating Miller Electric's 75th anniversary. Orange County Choppers designed and built the bike to commemorate the occasion and incorporated a patriotic

'Welding America' theme. The bike sported red, white and blue colours and featured a welding helmet morphing out of the gas tank, a mirror embedded in a MIG gun, a welding machine towed behind it and many other unique welding-related design elements. OCC is known for its patriotic bikes, including the Fire Bike, Jet Bike and the POW/MIA Bike. Based in Appleton, Wisconsin, Miller is the only manufacturer that produces all its arc welders and plasma

cutters in the United States, in a country where an estimated five to seven million Americans weld professionally or as a hobby.

The 2004 season premier of *American Chopper* was the highest ranked programme on cable TV among persons 25 to 54 years of age and the sixth most popular television show among men 18 to 34, having a total audience of 3.5 million viewers. The Miller 75th-anniversary chopper reportedly originated 'because of mutual respect between the companies. OCC owner Paul Teutul Sr. has used Miller welders for years and chief designer and fabricator Paul Teutul Jr. learned how to weld using a Millermatic all-in-one MIG welder. Miller invented this style of machine in 1971. Due to its affordability, ease of use and arc

performance, it has become a popular type of welder for light fabrication and home, hobbies, farm use and building motorcycles. The OCC shop exclusively uses Miller brand power sources and welding helmets. Early in 2003, Miller approached OCC with the modest request, 'Would OCC develop a 75th-anniversary design for a new auto-darkening welding helmet?', to which OCC responded, "Helmet? We want to build a bike. We always wanted to build a welding bike. '

Apart from welders, the machine that has probably had the most influence on the design of custom motorcycles in general and choppers in particular was the increasingly widespread use of the CNC milling machines used to make custom parts. Billet aluminium could be turned into any number of hitherto unmanufacturable components that allowed the style and quality of bikes to rapidly progress. Typically, on these new bikes, billet-aluminium was used to manufacture fork yokes, brake calipers, footpegs and shifters, wheel hubs, custom primary covers and more.

A window opened onto the Harley scene in the early 21st century when 100 years of Harley-Davidson history was celebrated on America's East Coast. A total of 36 members of the Eastern Harley-Davidson Dealers Association met for the largest Harley-Davidson celebration at Maple Grove Raceway. The association included dealers from Delaware, Maryland, New Jersey, Pennsylvania and Virginia. Here bikers and motorcycle enthusiasts could see the world's biggest and baddest nitro-burning Harleys, the most radical customs and

OPPOSITE and LEFT
A more conventional but no less classy
Sportster chopper from Phil Piper's
Chopper Shack. The Sportster tank, rigid
frame and chain drive certainly do much
to produce a 'chopper with attitude'.

PAGE 214
Two generations of chopper and chopper
builder. Custom painter Dark Star on his
nineties-style rigid with son Harley on
his 21st-century chopper. The duo call
themselves Bloodline Choppers.

restored antique bikes, as well as a head-to-toe tattooing contest, and could have a demonstration ride on the 2003 Harley-Davidsons. Daytona, Myrtle Beach, Sturgis and Laconia all celebrated the event as well as Milwaukee, where the factory hosted a major rider event in August 2003 to mark its official 100th-anniversary celebrations.

For the Discovery channel's *Biker Build-Off*, Billy Lane and the crew at Choppers Inc. built a heavily-detailed, Revtech-engined rigid called Misbehavin'. This bike beat Roger Bourget's creation and in a second round Billy Lane built a bike to compete with Cycle Fab's Dave Perewitz, a long-standing member of the Hamsters MC

custom bike club. The bikes were built and ridden from Florida to the *Easyriders* show in Dallas, Texas, where Lane was voted as the winner. He went on to build a bike for that year's Camel Roadhouse tour.

The distinctive sound of Harley-Davidson motorbikes was the topic of a speech, one of 42 on technical matters, at the

Most of the new generation of choppers are fitted with long but highly-engineered telescopic forks,

215

SAE Noise and Vibration Conference and Exhibition in Traverse City. Deane B. Jaeger, manager of Sound and Vibration Technology at Harley-Davidson, addressed a meeting of the Society of Automotive Engineers on 'The Acoustical History of Harley-Davidson'. SAE is a non-profit-making engineering and scientific organization dedicated to the advancement of mobility technology. The conference is the premier event for experts in passenger vehicle noise and vibration in the world, and attracts over 1,700 engineers and technical managers to northern Michigan from around the world.

The historical overview of Harley-Davidson included a look at a long line of air-cooled V-twin engines, beginning with the first V-twin in 1909 and progressing through the years to the Knucklehead, Panhead, Shovelhead and Blockhead designs. Over the past century the sound a Harley makes has been refined, but remains relatively unchanged in that it represents the heart and soul of an American icon. A tremendous amount of engineering was required to achieve the distinctive Harley sound, while meeting ever severe environmental regulations, though the expectations of customers and the community at large were taken into account. Jaeger shared some of the 'secrets' of establishing and maintaining a trademarked sound.

ABOVE
Eddie Trotta built this contemporary chopper for the Camel Roadhouse tour.

RIGHT
The new bikes have certainly extended the boundaries of both chopper engineering and styling. This bike combines numerous curved components into a stylish machine, with gas tank, exhaust pipes and frame downtube complementing each other.

Harley-Davidson Incorporated announced record revenue and earnings for its fourth quarter in the year ending 31 December 2003, which amounted to $1.16 billion compared with $1.03 billion the previous year, a 12.8 per cent increase. Net income for the quarter was $182.4 million compared with $150.9 million, an increase of 20.9 per cent over the same period. Fourth quarter diluted earnings per share (EPS) was 60 cents, a 22.4 per cent increase compared with the previous year's 49 cents. Revenue for the full year was $4.62 billion compared with $4.09 billion in 2002, a 13 per cent increase. Net income for the year was $760.9 million, a 31.1 per cent increase against the previous year's $580.2 million, while diluted EPS for the full year was $2.50, a 31.6 per cent increase compared with $1.90 in 2002.

This was the 18th consecutive year that Harley-Davidson has broken records for both revenue and net income. According to Jeffrey L. Bleustein, chairman and chief executive officer of Harley-Davidson. 'We had a phenomenal year full of memorable once-in-a-lifetime experiences surrounding our 100th Anniversary. Introducing the Harley-

Davidson brand to hundreds of thousands of potential customers has undoubtedly sparked the dream of ownership and created new excitement for our products. As we begin our 101st year, we expect to grow the business further with our proven ability to deliver a continuous stream of exciting new motorcycles, related products and services. We have set a new goal for the company to be able to satisfy a yearly demand of 400,000 Harley-Davidson motorcycles in 2007. By offering innovative products and services, and by driving productivity gains in all facets of our business, we are confident that we can deliver an earnings growth rate in the mid-teens for the foreseeable future.'

The fourth quarter results showed that revenue from Harley-Davidson motorcycles

Desperado is a company that offers these softail-type choppers off the peg.

RIGHT
Not unexpectedly, the new-style
choppers are to be seen everywhere
during Daytona Bikeweek.

OPPOSITE
Extreme Cycleworks offers these ready-
built choppers to customers. The tank-
mounted nitrous-oxide bottle ensures top
performance.

was $945.3 million, an increase of $125.0 million or 15.2 per cent over the same period the previous year. Shipments of motorcycles totalled 77,056 units, an increase of 11,086 units or 16.8 per cent over the previous year's fourth quarter, though the company's shipment target remained 317,000 Harley-Davidson motorcycles for 2004.

Revenue from genuine motor parts and accessories totalled $141.0 million, an increase of $11.1 million or 8.5 per cent, while revenue from general merchandise, consisting of apparel and collectibles, totalled $50.7 million, a decrease of $4.1 million or 7.4 per cent. Excluding revenue from the 100th-anniversary products in 2002's fourth quarter, the P&A growth rate

would have been 20.3 per cent over the previous year's fourth quarter and the general merchandise growth rate would have been 20.0 per cent over the same period. Gross margin was 35.9 per cent of revenue, down slightly from the previous year's 36.1 per cent. The gross margin was negatively impacted by a higher proportion of Sportster motorcycle shipments and

OPPOSITE
On the street in Hulett, Wyoming, during the Sturgis rally and races. Hulett is a short ride into Wyoming from South Dakota and is becoming increasingly popular as a place to ride to.

LEFT
Ron Simms, of Bay Area Custom Cycle, and the painter Horst have been around the custom bike scene for years, and skulls and flames have always been popular themes.

higher manufacturing costs, but was partially offset by favourable foreign currency exchange rates.

Retail sales of Harley-Davidson motorcycles for the year 2003 grew 8.8 per cent in the U.S., 6.7 per cent in Europe and 9.0 per cent in Japan compared with 2002. Based on the information then available, Harley-Davidson's full year market share for the 651-cc and upwards segment was expected to grow in all of the company's major markets. 'Given the economic climate during the past year, we are pleased with our retail growth,' said Bleustein. 'Although our U.S. dealer network experienced a modest decline in motorcycle sales in the fourth quarter as compared to last year's fourth quarter, we believe it is difficult to draw

OPPOSITE
Big Dog Motorcycles is one of the longest established suppliers of ready-built custom bikes and choppers.

ABOVE AND LEFT
Alan James of Black Bear Harley-Davidson with his modern-style chopper, built from the ground up in his garage in the old-style way.

meaningful conclusions from this comparison. The urgency to buy a 100th Anniversary motorcycle prior to the celebrations, along with an unusually late shipment plan for '04 motorcycles, created two very different selling environments. We are confident that 2004 will be another strong year for Harley-Davidson due to current dealer confidence, momentum from the 100th Anniversary and improving economic indicators.'

During the Sturgis Black Hills Rally of 2004 an exhibition of the photographer Michael Lichter's work was mounted in the museum in Rapid City, South Dakota. The exhibition was entitled *Kickstart: Art of the Chopper* and included a selection of choppers from Billy Lane, Arlin Fatland, Paul Yaffe, Mondo Porras and Arlen Ness. It was a popular display and attracted considerable attention. Discovery channel's *Biker Build-Off* of 2004 included ten bike-builders, ranging from some who'd been around for years, such as Indian Larry and Dave Perewitz, to newcomers like Mitch Bergeron and Joe Martin, while in between came Matt Hotch, Paul Yaffe, Kendall Johnson, Billy Lane, Chica and Russ Mitchell.

Harley-Davidson, the originator of the factory custom motorcycle, recognized the rapidly increasing popularity and mainstream acceptance of choppers and offered four new models for 2005, broadening its Sportster, Dyna Glide and Softail motorcycle lines with the introduction of the new models. 'This is an exciting model year,' said Bill Davidson, Harley-Davidson's director of marketing and

motorcycle product development. 'With four new models and a host of updates, Harley-Davidson's 2005 models demonstrate the company's continued leadership in factory custom styling. The soul of Harley-Davidson runs deeper than paint and chrome, and every 2005 model carries that unique strain of motorcycle DNA that's unmistakably and positively Harley-Davidson. It's a look and sound and just-right feeling that simply can't be duplicated.'

The new Softail models reinforced Harley-Davidson's position as masters of factory custom styling. The FLSTN/I Softail Deluxe and FLSTSC/I Softail Springer Classic both incorporated many nostalgic styling cues that blended seamlessly with the modern performance and comfort of the Harley-Davidson Softail platform, while the Dyna Glide family grew to five models with the introduction of the FXDC/I Super Glide Custom. The XL Sportster 883L motorcycle featured a lower seat height and adjusted ergonomics were designed to fit a wide range of riders and to make it easier to remove the bike from its sidestand.

All 2005 Sportster models had a new swing-arm and larger-diameter rear axle, while the VRSC V-Rod models were available in a greater range of colour options. The VRSCB was available in five colours, while the VRSCA model was offered in nine colour choices, including four two-tone combinations. A number of Softail, Touring, Dyna Glide and Sportster models were available with a sleek new chrome-aluminium profile laced wheel as an original-equipment option.

OPPOSITE
Darkside Choppers offers highly futuristic styling on bikes built in its shop but relies on some old-type components, such as springer forks (bottom picture).

LEFT
More restrained choppers are still being built and ridden in these first years of the 21st century, including this neat and uncluttered rigid Evo Sportster.

Harley-Davidson introduced 11 new paint combinations for 2005, including three new solid colours, two Sunglow Pearl shades and six new two-tone and three-tone combinations. Eleven of the 2005 models also featured new tank badges or decals. Prices for 2005 Harley-Davidson motorcycles start at $6,495 for an XL883 Sportster model, while the company's line of custom and touring bikes range from $6,495 to $20,405. Special limited-production models from the Custom Vehicle Operations programme range from $25,495 to $29,995.

Somewhere in between the shop-built, one-off choppers and factory-built stockers come outfits like Big Dog Motorcycles, Redneck Engineering, Big Daddy Choppers, Bourget's Bike Works, Echelon Motorcycle Co., Hellbound Steel Motorcycles, Midwest Choppers, Big Easy Choppers, Thunder Mountain Custom Cycles, Big Bear Choppers, Big Inch Bikes, Lifestyle Cycles, Swift Motorcycle Co., American Ironhorse Motorcycle Co., Titan Motorcycle Co., Milwaukee Motorcycle Co. and the Ultra Motorcycle Co.

Big Dog Motorcycles LLC of Wichita manufactures a line of heavyweight cruisers centred on a 107-ci (1750-cc) V-twin engine, the company selling its motorcycles across the United States through a growing number of authorized dealers. It is responsible for setting new standards in high-end, customized cruising motorcycles since its foundation in 1994. The company's corporate branding complements the sharp motorcycle design introduced in 2002, which evolved from its earlier retro styles. The new bikes

OPPOSITE and LEFT
As it did in the seventies, the Sportster engine offers the potential of a slim chopper. This rigid version features a modern wide back tyre beneath a custom rear fender and an array of carefully selected custom parts to enhance its simple lines.

PAGES 230, 231 and 232
Jesse James is one of the pioneers of the contemporary-style chopper. His new and radical styles of gas tank and exhaust pipes and the imaginative way his choppers are put together have brought him to the forefront of the chopper-building scene.

OPPOSITE
Many of these new-style choppers use rear wheels and tyres so wide that they need two pairs of bends in the rear portion of the frame to make then fit around the rear wheel.

feature 'Super Fat' (wide rear) tyres, radical
stretched frames and machined aluminium
wheels. 'Our new corporate logo captures our
spirit, everything Big Dog is about;
uncompromising quality, innovation, cutting-
edge motorcycles and a commitment to
growing our company,' says its president,
Nick Messer. 'It's a great way to kick off the
rollout of our 2003 models.'

The award-winning Gardner Design, also
of Wichita, developed the new look, which
updated the previous Big Dog winged logo
with a red 'B' within a silver 'D', conveying
power and motion. Below the initials is the
mechanically inspired type treatment of Big
Dog Motorcycles. 'Big Dog has an incredible
reputation for craftsmanship and attention to
detail,' says Gardner Design president, Bill
Gardner. 'The new image conveys that
simply, yet boldly.' Gardner explained that
his designers and Big Dog team members
worked together on a strategy to emphasize
the company's history and its future and to
acknowledge the people who ride Big Dog
motorcycles. They intend to build upon the
value of the Big Dog name, the better to
convey the company's new design styles. The
new identity will be applied to everything
from motorcycles to custom parts, clothing
and accessories.

In 2005 there is no limit to the range of
aftermarket parts being advertised nationally
and internationally. A glance through a
custom bike magazine reveals material from
Choppers Inc., Drag Specialties, RC
Components, Paul Yaffe Originals, Daytec,
Milwaukee Iron, Performance Machine Inc.,
U.S.A. Twins, Thunder Cycle Design, Hitech

OPPOSITE and LEFT
The long stretched gas tanks that run
from the headstock to the front of the
seat are almost de rigueur, but they serve
a practical purpose in styling the long-
frame top tube necessitated by the high
headstock.

Brothers, Arlen Ness, Samson, Ironworks Motorcycle Co., AMEN Motorcycles, Central Coast Cycles, Killer Chopper, Jim's, Patrick Racing, American Thunder, Rowe Performance, Comp Cams, Covington's Cycle City, Custom Cycle Engineering Co., Exile Cycles, Pro-1, Walz Hardcore Cycles, Products, Belt Drives Ltd., Xtreme Machine, Headwinds, Carolina Custom, Aeromach Manufacturing Inc., Envy Cycle Creations, Metry Custom Cycles, Baker Drivetrain, Mystery Designs, Tauer Machine, Sputhe Engineering, Wicked Image, Martin Brothers, Sumax, War Eagle, Carriage Work Inc., Fat Katz, RMD Billet, Sharper Wheels, Thompson Choppers Inc., Custom Chrome Inc., Paughco, Santee, Rolling Thunder Mfg., Mike Phillips' Grandeur Cycle, Ego Tripp, Pro-One Performance Manufacturing Inc., Corbin, Vance and Hines, S&S, Le Pera, Edelbrock, Küryakyn, Crane Cams, Wicked

Fog Hollow, BMC Choppers, Hurricane Customs, Exotic Choppers, Hertland U.S.A., Atlas Precision, Sculpture Cycles, Joker Machine, Killer Clown, Zippers, MGS Custom Bikes, Paramount Custom Cycles, Landmark, Hallcraft, JP Cycles, Wilwood and at least as many again. From this list it is

OPPOSITE AND BELOW
American Ironhorse is another of the major builders of off-the-shelf choppers and, like the others, trades from a huge display unit at Sturgis and Daytona.

PAGE 238
Whatever style of bike you're riding
there'll be a cold beer waiting at
Daytona's Boot Hill Saloon.

PAGES 239, 240 and 241
Ultra Motorcyles of California is
another supplier of ready-built choppers,
a market which is currently booming in
the U.S.A. These bikes are built
completely from parts available through
the custom aftermarket.

clear that many of the long-established companies are still in business but that many new ones are supplying the almost limitless demand for custom parts and shop-built choppers.

This trend towards shop-built choppers to satisfy an unprecedented mass market isn't to everyone's taste, of course, and long-time chopper riders would have been heartened, no doubt, to read Beatnik's comments concerning an old-school rigid springer Sportster chop, in the November 2004 edition of *Biker* magazine. He wrote, 'In today's world of catalogue-built, bolt-on customs and high-dollar designer bullshit bikes, to see some good, old-fashioned hard work done by the owner in his own garage with attention to detail and respect for the past are rare commodities indeed.' However, the journey isn't over yet. Not by a long way.

CHAPTER SEVEN
CHOPPER PEOPLE

Keith 'Bandit' Ball at his workstation, from which he runs his international biker web site. His glass-topped table is a unique creation and incorporates a Panhead engine and springer forks.

A chopper is a motorcycle. It is a mode of transport, a rolling piece of metal sculpture, a statement, a way of life. With its origins going back 60 years or more, the technique of chopping a bike has evolved over the years. Just as each decade can be defined by changing fashions in clothing and hairstyles, for example, so too have choppers changed. Choppers themselves have been in and out of fashion over the years – admired by many but ridden by few. They were once regarded as the province of the outlaw, someone who rejected the status quo, a free spirit. This positive sense of separation from mainstream society is what is known as the 'chopper attitude', though being an uncompromising ride, the chopper is not for everyone.

Attitudes change, however, and with ever-expanding TV cable and satellite channels competing for viewers, even fringe activities such as building custom bikes and hot rodding cars are now open to scrutiny. Such is the power of television that different ways of living beyond the experience of the masses are brought into their homes, and this includes the world of choppers. This

particular lifestyle has now been repackaged for public consumption, demonstrating that bikers and chopper-builders can be interesting and intelligent human beings, the majority being outlaws no longer but taken from a wide section of society as a whole.

Television creates its own heroes, such as the aptly-named modern chopper-builder, Jesse James, a relative of the James brothers, who once blazed their own trail across the West. The popularity of the reality TV show, *American Chopper*, is unprecedented, bringing choppers and the colourful characters associated with them to millions of homes across the U.S.A.

The patriotic themes that inspire the Teutuls are particularly popular with an American audience and the family's appearance on the Jay Leno *Tonight* show demonstrates a level of public acceptance never accorded to the chopper/biker world before. Moreover, a demand for chopper-style V-twins was simultaneously created, the like of which never existed in the past. Chopper-building is now a multi-billion-dollar market with countless companies supporting an ever-increasing demand.

Below are some profiles of Chopper People – some famous, some unknown, but all with a story to tell. Mike Parti, a 70-year- old who once belonged to the Galloping Gooses motorcycle club, whose members liked nothing better than to raise hell on their bobbers, provides an insight into the early days of the chopper, while the Martin brothers, young builders now in the process of forming their own style, are looking confidently to the future.

Included are builders from Japan, France, Germany and Great Britain, the millionaire chopper-builders rubbing shoulders with the back-street chopper enthusiasts: all have something to say on the subject of what this chopper thing is all about.

KEITH RANDALL BALL

Keith Randall Ball has been an influential figure in the world of bikers and chopped Harleys for over 30 years. For much of that time he has been working on the biker lifestyle magazine, *Easyriders*, initially as a staff writer and manager of ABATE since issue No. 3 in 1971, and rising to editor and finally vice-president and editorial director of the parent company. Today he writes biker fiction and runs a busy web site for the Harley biker on www.bikernet.com.

The influence of *Easyriders* magazine on the American biker cannot be overestimated. There had been other magazines before it, dedicated to the

Keith is surrounded by mementoes of his life in the world of bikes. This Knucklehead chopper sits beneath an oil painting of Keith astride the very same machine.

chopper scene, such as *Street Chopper*, *Chopper*, *Big Bike* and *Supercycle*, none of which managed to strike the right note. The cover line of *Easyriders* once read: 'For the Swinging Biker', but this was soon replaced by 'Entertainment for Adult Bikers'.

It was conceived by three *paisanos*, Mil Blair, Joe Teresi and Lou Kimzey. They were all chopper riders and builders, totally devoted to the biker scene, and were also involved in various bike magazines in the late sixties. In short, they had all the credentials and a great idea for a ground-breaking new biker lifestyle magazine. The rest is history. *Easyriders* is still the best-selling motorcycle magazine on the planet

and a number of foreign-language editions are also published.

Keith entered this crazy world more by luck than design. He had completed three tours of Vietnam, where he had been serving in the U.S. Navy. He already had a custom-painted Sportster, which he had loaned out to a friend. This he replaced with an ex-police 1966 Shovelhead, which was the first bike he took to pieces and began to customize. At the same time he landed a job at a custom bike shop in the Long Beach area of California called U.S. Choppers. He possessed some mechanical skills but probably not enough for the job, but his persistence paid off. It was Keith's opinion

that the shop was run by a couple of crazies who didn't treat their customers right, and he wanted out.

He had been helping a friend build a Knucklehead when the first edition of *Easyriders* hit the news-stands. He noticed that it was published in Seal Beach, ten miles from Long Beach where he lived. Having nothing to lose, he wrote to the editor, Lou Kimzey, telling him about the nice old Knucklehead he might like to feature. Lou only lived a couple of miles away, so he rode over to take a look and Keith rode to meet him on his 1966 Shovel, which he had put in a rigid frame, though it was somewhat rough and ready. Lou liked the Knucklehead, but liked the rigid better and offered to feature Keith's bike too, having a liking for ratty-looking old chops. At that time, Keith was the archetypal 'scummy' biker: long hair, matted beard and covered in motorcycle oil and grease.

But Lou must have liked what he saw and heard because he invited Keith over to the *Easyriders* office and offered him a job as manager of ABATE, an organization which *Easyriders* had already set up to lobby government on bikers' rights. At that time ABATE stood for A Brotherhood Against Totalitarian Enactments, but today it means A Brotherhood Aimed Toward Education, which possibly sounds more positive. But it was a visionary idea which, with Keith Ball at the helm, quickly caught on all over America.

It should be appreciated that but for the creation of ABATE chapters across America, the whole custom bike and chopper scene

OPPOSITE
Keith loves old-timers, such as this Harley springer Panhead dating back to 1948.

BELOW LEFT
He has a cherished bike in every room of his house and many pictures and artefacts such as this 'wire and weld' chopper sculpture.

245

would have been outlawed by government and only stock motorcycles would have been legal. ABATE successfully demonstrated that chopped long-fork motorcycles were not inherently unstable and that provided certain guidelines were followed, quite safe enough, with the result that the anti-motorcycle modification laws was effectively brought to an end in the U.S.A.

Keith took ABATE from 500 to 28,000 members across 30 states in less than ten years. It has been vociferous in its rejection of compulsory helmet laws in the U.S.A. and has succeeded in repealing the law in many states, which shows that provided one is organized and protests *en masse*, governments and local authorities are more likely to listen and respect one's rights.

At the same time that Keith was developing ABATE, he was writing features on custom bikes and rising through the ranks. He was also a member of an outlaw club – the hardest of the hard – and knew what loyalty to a club and a sense of brotherhood meant. One could say that Keith has talked the talk and walked the walk, whether on the streets or in the publishing world. Like most men he has mellowed with the passing years, but the outlaw spirit is still there lurking beneath the surface.

Now he has left the magazine publishing world, been there, seen it all, done it all, and his full attention is given to the world of the internet. Working from his home by the sea, surrounded by the memorabilia of his life, not to mention a motorcycle in every room, he interacts with the biker world he helped to protect.

ROGER BOURGET

Roger Bourget's father served in the U.S.A.F. and owned an old military 45-ci WLA, so his son was familiar with Harley-Davidsons when he was still quite young. These old Harleys were slow but youngsters have the need to go fast, so Roger became involved with dirt bikes and raced in motocross throughout his high-school years before progressing to a series of street bikes.

Roger eventually became one of the main designers in the engineering department of Sea Ray boats, where he developed the skills and knowledge he would apply in a very different world later on. He acquired a

OPPOSITE
Keith likes nothing more than to blast around the seaport area of San Pedro, California, where he lives.

BELOW LEFT
The flame-decorated rear fender sports the Bourget Bike Works logo.

LEFT
The Bourget 'drop-seat' tubular construction is an unmistakable signature style.

1984 Harley Softail custom, and it is no surprise that the engineer in him would not permit him to leave the bike alone and soon he was tearing it down, raking it out and applying chrome and custom paint. This was the first of a string of personal project bikes, which included the first Harley custom to sport a 170-17 tyre at the rear.

Roger began to design and build his own frames out of his own garage, the demand for which grew until Bourget Bike Works was established and quickly became one of the largest constructors of custom bikes in the world today. Operating out of a 36,000-sq ft (3344-m²) facility in Phoenix, Arizona, the company produces a range of custom bikes and sells thousands of units a year.

OPPOSITE
The drop-seat design is achieved by storing the engine oil inside the frame, thus dispensing with the conventional under-seat oil tank

LEFT
The large-diameter frame tubes are unmistakably Bourget. This frame has rear suspension in the form of a hidden softail-style suspension unit.

It is true to say that a Bourget-framed custom bike is the most distinctive on the streets today. Bourget's beefy tubular frame designs, with their unmistakable wraparound rear sections, are unique. One gets the impression that the frame is indestructible, in that it appears both industrial and functional. The frame is the basis for any style of custom bike, of course, but no other manufacturer creates frames that are the most striking feature of the whole build.

Bourget's frame is protected and patented. He calls it his Oil in frame/Drop-seat style. Because the lubrication oil is stored in the tubular frame, the conventional oil tank has been discarded. The usual place for an oil tank is under the seat pan, but with Bourget's design the seat can be lowered to such an extent that the rider feels he is skimming the asphalt. The rider appears to be riding within the bike rather than perched on top of it. On the road, the Bourget bike is a perfect union of man and machine and is a true signature style.

The drop frame has been the basis for a range of model types, the most extreme example being the T6 Billet Retro chopper. This, as the name suggests, is constructed from aircraft-quality T6 6061 aluminium, hand-polished to a mirror finish and decorated with tribal designs or flames. It has a futuristic appearance, and with a hand-formed 'stealth'-style gas tank the Retro chopper is a rigid with an extreme extended springer front end. The sum of $70,000 gets you riding in exclusive style as each bike can be modified and personalized according to the customer's requirements.

After more than ten years in the business, an ever-increasing model range is now available, such as the Black Jack, Low Blow, Python Chopper, Beach Cruiser and Magnum Fat Daddy. The 11th-anniversary Magnum Fat Daddy is a tarmac-tearing street bike built for speed freaks. It has a 124-ci (2000-cc) S&S engine, a six-speed transmission, a Bourget inverted front end and a 280 rear tyre. The gas tank is designed to accommodate two chromed narrow bottles, one on either side, which means just one thing – nitrous oxide! This Bourget bike is certainly fast and furious. Rather like Roger's trademark Mohawk haircut, a Bourget bike stands out from the crowd like no other custom motorcycle in existence.

OPPOSITE
This bike would not be out of place on the drag strip – everything about it screams performance.

LEFT
To celebrate its 45th year in business, S&S produced a monster 145-ci (2376-cc) motor, following which a select group of customizers were given these motors and invited to build 45th-anniversary specials.

BELOW
This is the Retro chopper and is the most radical model in Bourget's range. The frame is of aircraft-quality aluminium and the tank is hand-formed, while the extended springer front end provides the retro touch.

NICOLAS CHAUVIN

Nicolas Chauvin, a Frenchman based in Paris, is one of the pre-eminent builders of custom Harleys in Europe. Surprisingly, this talented individual does not build bikes for a living but out of an artist's passion and need to create. He does all the work himself, down to the detailed paintwork for which he is particularly renowned. With his attention to detail and meticulous approach bordering on the obsessive, a Chauvin bike can take up to two years to complete, which is probably why he is not the most prolific of builders, but his creations sweep the board wherever they are shown.

Probably the most famous of his bikes is the tribute to Stevie Ray Vaughan, which is long, low and sleek, with painstakingly detailed artwork. It is much admired and sparked a whole new style in Europe. He took the bike to the Kent Custom Bike Show and beat the best the British could offer, running away with Best European, Best Paint, Best Engineering, Best Brightwork, Best Chopper and, naturally enough, Best in Show. When London's Barbican Art Gallery mounted the exhibition, *The Art of the Harley*, featuring some of the world's top customs, Stevie Ray, needless to say, was there.

The bike is based around a 1980 Shovelhead motor with Delkron crankcase, Andrews lifter blocks, Rivera cams and twin plugged heads for a more even burn in the cylinders. A Dell'Orto carburettor feeds the gas and air to the engine, while a Chauvin-

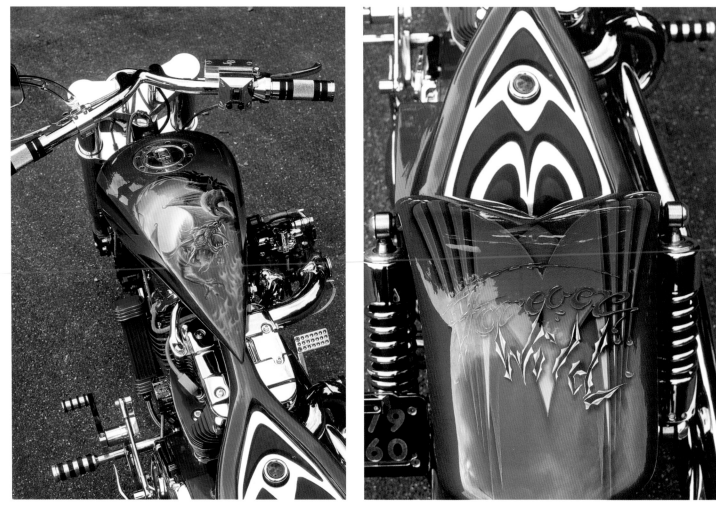

built exhaust takes care of the waste gases.

It is the frame that dictates the lines of a chopper and Chauvin has produced a one-off that is lower than stock, with a raked headstock that kicks the front wheel out. The forks are Kayaba upside-downs and the front wheel is from a Suzuki GSXR, while brakes from a GSXR are used front and back. When Stevie Ray was built, car wheels were the only way to go if a large rear tyre was required.

Chauvin is not unknown in the U.S.A., as one of his bikes, Demon in Paradise, achieved Best in Show in Daytona. When asked to explain his approach, he admits to a love of feminine shapes and likes his bikes to be rounded yet pointed, soft but also aggressive, with hot and cold tones. He regards his bikes as painted, travelling sculptures, designed to achieve an harmonious balance between colour and shape, with special attention paid to the way shapes and parts relate to one another.

Because Nicolas does not build bikes for profit, he is artistically free to spend as much time as he wishes on the small details. He sets himself no deadlines: the bike is finished when he feels it is finished and not before. This is why his standards are so high and why other builders swallow nervously when they hear he is ready to launch another example of his rolling art onto the custom-show arena.

OPPOSITE
LEFT and RIGHT
Nicolas is a professional graphic artist and designs and paints all the artwork on his bikes himself. Close inspection reveals how accomplished he really is.

BELOW LEFT
This Sportster-engined custom is called Forever Wild and was built by Nicolas for his partner Geraldine.

Chica is Japan's most famous chopper artist. Based in California, no more than a dozen one-off commissions are produced each year.

CHICA

While many chopper-builders are growing more futuristic in style, even venturing into the world of science fiction, there are others who are looking to the past for inspiration. Neither the old-school choppers of the sixties nor even the post-war bobbers can satisfy these retro-visionaries. Some are looking back even further, to the flat-track bikes of the 1930s, to the pared-to-the-bone racers, while some are looking to the Indian and Harley eight-valve racers of the early 1920s.

Nowhere is this trend more apparent than in the land of Honda, Suzuki and Kawasaki. Japan's premier chopper magazine, *Vibes*, is packed with the coolest examples of the style. The Japanese absolutely love the retro look, utilizing old flatheads and Knuckleheads and adapting and mixing the styles of yesteryear to create a whole new chopper genre. In fact, they are re-creating the old-style engineering, where all the working parts were on show. But these are very much alive in the present and the smell of hot oil and brake linings emanating from the bikes, parked up after a run, is sharply evocative.

Retro chopper shops are proliferating in Japan, the most famous being Zero Engineering. Around 1998, a disciple of the

Chica was inspired by the mythical unicorn when he came up with the concept for this bike, which he completed in 30 days for Discovery channel's Biker Build-Off.

movement arrived in California. Yasuyoshi 'Chica' Chikazawa, even though he was unable to speak English, was aware that to succeed as a master builder he would have to prove himself in the United States. Chica must have believed in himself to have transported himself and his wife and family from their homeland to an unfamiliar culture. Prior to this upheaval Chica lived in Kyoto, where he worked as a Honda mechanic while dreaming of Harleys. He was able to start up his own company, Chica Motorcycle Service, which serviced and repaired Harleys in particular but did little in the way of custom work.

Chica had a friend with a motorcycle shop in Diamond Bar, California, and it was there that he worked during his first 18 months in America. He then decided to strike out on his own, working from home for six months until the business grew sufficiently for him to establish Chica Custom Cycles in

OPPOSITE
LEFT and RIGHT
The swooping lines and curves of the
hand-built gas tank are complemented by
the gooseneck frame. The springer front
end and Shovelhead motor are from
different eras but have been combined by
Chica in his own inimitable style.

LEFT
The Primo primary belt drive is a
favoured aftermarket part utilized by
many chopper builders.

OPPOSITE
The heritage of the 1920s board-track racing bike is evident in this ironhead Sportster-powered creation by Chica.

FAR LEFT
The sleek pared-to-the-bone lines of this street racer are accentuated by the angle of this view. The trumpet-style megaphone exhausts have been plucked from the fifties.

LEFT
Chica favours the older Harley engines for their functional mechanical look. This ironhead Sportster engine is fitted with an SU constant-velocity carburettor.

Huntingdon Beach, California, where he has gradually begun to realize his dream and develop into the artist he undoubtedly is. Chica takes his inspiration from old bikes of the thirties, bobbers of the forties and fifties, and combines them with touches of seventies psychedelia. He likes to work with period parts, whenever possible, but when it comes to a Knucklehead-based project for a customer, will use a replica of the 1947 engine that is built by Flathead Power in Sweden. This company uses modern

metallurgy and has eliminated the weak spots in the old design to create totally reliable 'old' engines.

However, Chica does sometimes use modern Harley-style engines, but generally prefers the look of the Knuckles, Pans and Shovels. He fabricates many of his own parts and is skilled at taking old parts and re-modelling them to suit his intentions.

The orange bike opposite is called the Rumbler and is an example of the 1959 bobber style but has a seventies generator

Shovelhead motor combined with a forties-style springer front end. The handlebars are clip-ons, which give the bike an exciting, racy appearance. Chica's choppers utilize hardtail frames which have exaggerated 'gooseneck' front tubes typical of seventies choppers, while the Invader-style wheels of the period complete the seventies look.

Chica has unusually chosen a modern V-twin engine as well as a modern inverted front suspension for the bike illustrated below, which he calls Mighty Quick. These

modern features are combined with a hardtail frame and curiously old-fashioned megaphone exhausts.

Chica has evolved his own inimitable style which not only can be seen on Discovery channel's *Biker Build-Off* but also on the covers and centre spreads of chopper magazines throughout the world. Most satisfying of all is the fact that many of his bikes have been bought by Japanese collectors who have returned them to the land of his birth.

OPPOSITE
Once again Chica has selected features from different eras and combined them in this bike christened the Rumbler. It is part fifties bobber, part thirties racer and is powered by a seventies Shovelhead motor.

BELOW LEFT
Chica's bike, Mighty Quick, a combination of modern features married to a hardtail frame and old-fashioned megaphone exhausts.

DEE CLARK (New York Yankee Bike)
Dee Clark is the proprietor of a new custom bike shop called Ultimate Cycles of Newburgh, New York. He is a fanatical supporter of the New York Yankees and wished to create a tribute bike in honour of his beloved team. At one time he worked for Orange County Choppers, New York, so themed bikes were familiar territory to him;

he also figured that, as far as publicity was concerned, the project could do his fledgling business nothing but good.

Dee based his project on a Bourget rigid frame which had a steel front section and a bolt-on aluminium hardtail. The frame has 6 inches (15.25cm) in the downtube and the frame is also stretched 6in, with a rake of 45°. The classic long-forked look is achieved

with a Bourget 12-in (30.5-cm) over springer fork and there are three-spoked wheels from Weld Racing, the rear sporting a 240 Metzeler tyre. The gas tank is an Eddie Trotta creation, slightly modified and decorated with a Yankee logo engraved onto the flush-mounted gas cap.

The fenders were sourced from Russ Wernimont, while the oil tank is a Bourget-

OPPOSITE
Dee Clark sits proudly on his tribute to his favourite baseball team, the New York Yankees.

BELOW LEFT
The Yankees bike has a Bourget Bike Works frame and extended springer front end.

ABOVE

Close inspection reveals New York Yankees logos in hidden places such as here behind the headstock.

ABOVE RIGHT

The Danny Gray seat is stitched in baseball fashion while the stoplight shows NY in red.

FAR RIGHT

The wheels are three-spokes by Weld Racing.

made horseshoe shape bearing the words New York.

Dee naturally wanted the bike to appear as if it were dressed in Yankee kit and to this end commissioned Nub Graphix of Walden, New York, to apply a snow-white metallic paint finished with electric-blue stripes. Even the seat, a Danny Gray product, is made to resemble a baseball. It takes time to spot all the references to the New York Yankees that are incorporated into the design. They appear on the foot controls, the rear light, the gas cap, the rear-axle covers and the points cover; but the most important feature, of course, is the paint job.

The bike is powered by an S&S 113-ci (1850-cc) unit built by Bourget Bike Works. Super G carbs, topped by a velocity stack, breathe oxygen into the mill, while Dee's own short dragster pipes exhale the waste gases. A suicide clutch pedal disengages the Boyce clutch and a baseball bat-shaped hand shift selects the appropriate gear from the six available. Other accessories – headlight, handlebars and risers – are from Ted's V-Twin, while footpegs and foot controls are by Bourget Bike Works.

Even though he is a genuine Yankee fan, Dee could see that such a bike could be paraded in the Yankee Stadium to his advantage, which would also get it on TV, giving him the valuable publicity his business needed. In this he was successful: the first time the bike appeared at a World Series game, Yankees vs the Marlins, it created a public disturbance. As the fans went crazy, trying to get in on the act, it seemed as though the situation was about to get out of control, which the cops did not like one bit, and Dee was ordered to get the hell out or the bike would be impounded.

Even rival baseball fans love the bike, telling Dee 'we hate the Yankees but we love your chopper'. He loves to take the bike wherever there are Yankee fans, attending charity events with it and riding it in Little League baseball parades. The kids love the fact that the spark-plug wires are neon and have dual baseball bats built into each, which light up as the ignition fires.

Unfortunately, there is no fairy-tale ending to this story. The Yankees failed to take the 2004 World Series – beaten by the Boston Red Sox who hadn't won for over 80 years! Dee will therefore have to wait a while for the big parade through the streets of New York.

These short upturned exhaust pipes are more commonly seen on top-fuel dragster Harleys and are guaranteed to be heard all over the Yankee Stadium.

OPPOSITE
Jerry and David Covington alongside their show-winning creation, Lucifer.

RIGHT
The decoration of the chrome tank is evocative of a fifties car-hood ornament and is combined with old-school hot-rod pinstriping. The Panhead engine is a modern creation by Accurate Engineering and is a whopping 103ci (1688cc).

BELOW
A beautiful exercise in symmetry is achieved by the use of left- and right-hand dual carbs. The drop handlebars suggest a head-down racing position.

JERRY COVINGTON

Covington Cycle City of Woodward, Oklahoma, has been operating since 1993. It is run by Jerry Covington and his wife Kathleen, but in recent times his son, David, has been involved, building show-winning bikes himself. In fact, the bike shown here and overleaf – Lucifer – is mainly David's creation and recently impressed the judges in the 2004 Texas Chop-Off at the Lone Star Biker Bash, running away with Best in Show and a fat cheque for $30,000.

Jerry became interested in choppers in California during the early seventies. In those days, a number of businesses specialized in building long forks, stretched frames and all the parts the chopper rider of the period

The alignment of the huge 300 rear tyre is facilitated by the use of a Baker right-side drive six-speed gearbox.

could possibly need, while Arlen Ness, Ron Simms, Bob Dron, Barry Cooney and Denver's Choppers, among others, were developing the movement that had been kick-started by the film *Easy Rider* in 1969.

Chopper riders still did much of the bike construction themselves, maybe buying in a frame and wheels and sourcing or adapting other parts to fit. Denver's Choppers was one of the businesses whose frames were in great demand. Jerry liked to go over to to its works in Riverside and talk to whoever was hanging out – comparing bikes and swapping parts and ideas. Jerry loved hardtail frames with long springer front ends, what everyone today would refer to as 'old-school'.

Jerry thought a chopper should be as minimalist as possible, having only what was needed to make it go and stop. Like many custom builders he was also into the hot-rod scene, and was actually in the business of building custom cars for many years while knocking out a chopper or two at regular intervals. When he arrived in Oklahoma from California in 1993, he intended to carry on building cars for a living, but became sidetracked, as is often the case, when he built a chopper for himself. Someone immediately wanted to buy it and Covington Cycle City was up and running.

Any customer buying a Covington bike can be sure that there has been meticulous attention to detail and an impeccable finish. It is not enough that a bike looks good on the surface. Jerry prides himself on the fact that areas not immediately visible – the underside of the tank, under the seat, etc. – are as well finished as every other part of the bike. In his

opinion, a chopper should have good flowing lines and harmony of form – a sculpture in metal and paint – while never forgetting that it is a vehicle, a mode of transport. It must fulfil this role and provide the rider with a truly great riding experience, without which it is worthless.

Large-capacity motors are commonly installed in Jerry's bikes, often of 124ci (2000cc). Such a high-powered outfit is not strictly necessary for cruising on a chopper, but people like to know they have plenty of power in reserve, which is sometimes necessary to rescue a rider from a bad situation by offering a way of escape.

The future of Covington Cycle City is looking good now that David Covington is turning out such radical bikes as Lucifer. For this he took a Covington 300 Sinner frame with a custom downtube drilled out like that of an early race bike. With its low stance and Paughco springer front end, it is reminiscent of the Bay Area Low Riders of the late seventies. It is powered by a 103-ci (1688-cc) Panhead motor by Accurate Engineering, breathing through dual Stromberg 97 carburettors, one on each side of the motor, with slash-cut vertical stacks creating positive air pressure through the carbs. The engine exhales through a Covington exhaust, which has the look of a megaphone, while the transmission is a Baker right-side drive six-speed. This gearbox is the darling of the custom builder because, with rear tyre sizes growing to 330, more room is needed to align the motor and rear wheel. Big-twin motors have their chain- or belt-drive on the left-hand side of the bike; as the fashion for

huge rear tyres grew, motors literally had to be offset in the frame to line up the final drives, which compromised the balance and handling. The Baker transmission, with its right-side drive, enables the builder to keep the motor in line with the frame and rear-wheel axis.

The bike runs on Covington Corleone wheels. The extreme low-to-the-ground effect is possible because a Legend Air Ride system has been fitted. This is a popular option as it is an adjustable compressed-air

system that raises and lowers the ride height of the bike. This is controlled by the rider, who selects the lowest setting for cruising down Main Street because the 'slammed-to-the-ground' look is cool. Higher ride level can then be selected for normal highway use and enables safe cornering clearance. David Covington is set to make a big impression on the custom bike scene if this is any indication of his talent.

The dual Stromberg carbs are fed pressurized air due to the forward-facing slash-cut billet stacks.

ARLIN FATLAND

By his own admission, Arlin Fatland is 'just an old-town farm boy'. Farming was not to be the future of the young Arlin, however. His parents had forbidden him a motorcycle and he was forced to look on enviously as the coolest guy in his small home town tore up and down on a stroked Sportster, impressing all the girls. Arlin needed some space and some action, so he ran away to the city of Denver, Colorado, in the early sixties. There he acquired a couple of old British pre-unit Triumphs – 'kind of ugly old choppers with apehangers'.

In the mid-sixties Arlin enjoyed running around Denver on his Triumph chopper and eventually got a job selling and fixing Japanese bikes. But he was not the type to work for a boss and figured he could do

OPPOSITE
Arlin Fatland is one of the founding fathers of the Hamsters, an exclusive club of master bike-builders.

LEFT
This hardtail springer has 120-spoke wheels and a cut-down Indian-style rear fender. Arlin loves to confuse and amuse so he fitted an Xzotic Panhead rocker cover on the front cylinder and an Xzotic Knucklehead cover on the rear.

BELOW
Dual Edelbrock carbs supply fuel and air to the mill.

better himself. In 1970, he opened up his own bike shop and Two-Wheelers of Denver was born. By 1974 Arlin and his crew had a serious business on their hands, concentrating mainly on Harleys because that is where the money was.

It was around this time that Arlin and his friends rode up to Sturgis. They decided not to go the more direct route through Wyoming because the state had just introduced a helmet law and there was no way they would wear them. So they took the long way round, through Nebraska and north to South Dakota. This added an extra two days to the trip, but they had the wind in their hair, knees in the breeze, hanging onto those apehangers.

OPPOSITE
Arlin aboard his latest bike, the Gambler, the perfect chopper for going from bar to bar.

ABOVE
Arlin complements the bike with his matching cowboy boots.

LEFT
The scalloped paint job and colour-matched air filter and rocker covers are neat touches.

RIGHT
Maltese-cross mirrors, pullback bars and sprung solo seat are all old-school style.

FAR RIGHT
The scallop paint job is continued on the rear fender along with a pair of lucky dice.

OPPOSITE
In the late seventies Arlin was building Bay Area Low Riders of which these two are perfect examples.

PAGE 278
This Knucklehead bobber, built by Arlin many years ago, echoes many of the features seen on his latest chopper, the Gambler, such as a scalloped paint job, Sportster tank, cut-back curved rear fender and boomerang fender strut.

Those were the crazy old days of City Park, where all kinds of action was allowed and the police made themselves scarce. Arlin got his kicks in the world of crazy bikers and chopped Harleys, but he was also gaining an insight into what was required by people wanting to build their own. People like Arlen Ness, Dave Perewitz and Barry Cooney were building chopped Harleys and entering them in custom shows in Sturgis and elsewhere, indicating that building a show-winning custom bike was a good way of advertising a bike shop and show-casing newly-designed parts into the bargain.

So the die was cast, Arlin laying down his challenge to the master builders, and pretty soon became one of them, hanging out

with the top U.S. bike-builders, chatting and drinking beer.

Arlin figures that it was during one of these beer-soaked evenings that the idea of the Hamsters was born. No one can remember whose idea it actually was, but the Hamsters has since evolved into a club for master bike-builders, with membership by invitation only. Members can be identified at events by the distinctive yellow T-shirts bearing a cartoon hamster. Why yellow? According to Arlin it is 'so we could spot each other among all the black biker T-shirts, I guess'.

Arlin still owns 20 to 30 bikes which he has built over the years. He is not sure of the exact number, as he keeps finding bikes he has forgotten covered in tarpaulins and dust.

Some of the early show-winners were built around 1979–80 and were Bay Area Low Riders. Others called them 'diggers', pioneered by San Francisco builders Arlen Ness and Ron Simms. They were often based on Sportster engines, with spindly hardtail frames with prism- or coffin-shaped gas tanks and even spindlier springer front ends. Engines and other metal parts were often engraved and gold-plated, while paint jobs utilized gold leaf to create swirly patterns. These diggers were low, narrow and long, built for show rather than go.

Today, in addition to his shop on 38th Avenue, Denver, Arlin has others in both main streets of Sturgis and Daytona Beach, venues that attract the biggest biker gatherings in the U.S.A., both having been established for more than 60 years.

Arlin's custom bikes appear to have no identifiable style, unlike those of most other builders, whose creations can more often than not be immediately recognized. Arlin is a law unto himself and builds anything he feels like in whatever style that takes his fancy. Every year he builds a couple of show bikes which are always different from anything that has gone before. Unusual parts often find their way into his workshop, which may trigger him into saying, 'Hell, yeah, lets build a bike around this'. You just never know what he will think of next.

All three of his shops sell an eclectic mix of old-school parts and accessories, collectibles and curiosities. His partner, Donna, designs and sells high-quality leather goods, making the Two-Wheelers shops veritable Aladdin's caves compared with the ones which surround them that sell identical T-shirts and not much else.

Gold leaf, gold-plating and engraving are all features characteristic of the choppers of the late seventies and early eighties, and not often seen on the choppers of today.

Horst airbrushing one of his trademark skull designs onto a gas tank.

HORST

Horst is the painter of choice of Ron Simms (see page 376). He is a veteran of the Bay Area scene of the sixties and living proof that if you remember what you got up to in the sixties you weren't there! Needless to say, Horst doesn't remember a lot. A very private man, he shuns publicity, but he did give this interview and this is what he had to say:

'In about 1969 I had a motorcycle and took the tank off to get it painted. The guy had it for about three weeks and didn't get in finished. It was the middle of summer and I wanted to go riding, so I took the tank back

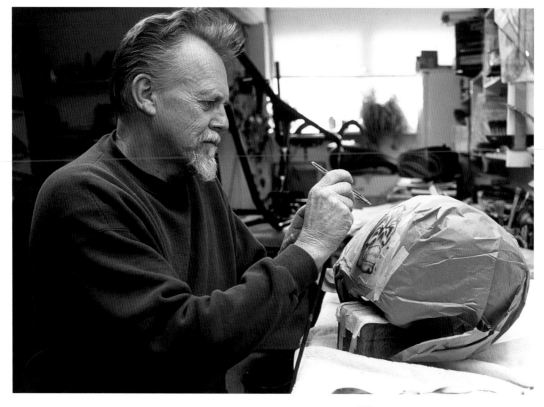

and got a spray can and painted some flames on it. It looked like shit so I repainted it again and again. Then it looked pretty good so I started painting some friends' bikes and it just kinda snowballed and became a living. I like painting motorcycles, I always have. It's a small area: it's not like a car where you spend weeks on it. I've painted some cars, vans and trucks, you name it. I've painted a few Corvettes and a couple of boats. I painted an airplane for a guy, a Cessna, painted it different colours. But motorcycles are kinda the mainstay.

'The late sixties here in San Francisco? Man, we just had a blast. A lot of drugs, a lot of drinking, a lot of whatever goes along with it – a lot of partying. I've had my paint shops in this area for the last thirty-odd years. I spent most of the seventies riding motorcycles, and the first half of the eighties. I still ride once in a while, I kinda slowed down a little bit, other things to life, but I still enjoy being on a motorcycle. These days I've got a 1990 Harley-Davidson Springer. I'm not crazy about the Springer front end but it's a nice bike.

'I bought the bike in about 1992 or so, I got it from a guy who quit riding it when they passed the helmet laws, so I got the bike pretty cheap, rode it about for a year or so, and then I thought I'd do a quickie paint job. I was doing a set of flames for a guy, so I just painted the same flames on my bike and never got round to repainting it.

'Yeah, ghost flames were popular even thirty years ago. I used to use Murano Pearl; it was real pearl. The skull thing is more recent. I painted a few of them back in the

Ron Simms' bikes are famed for their skull and flame paint jobs, all provided courtesy of Horst.

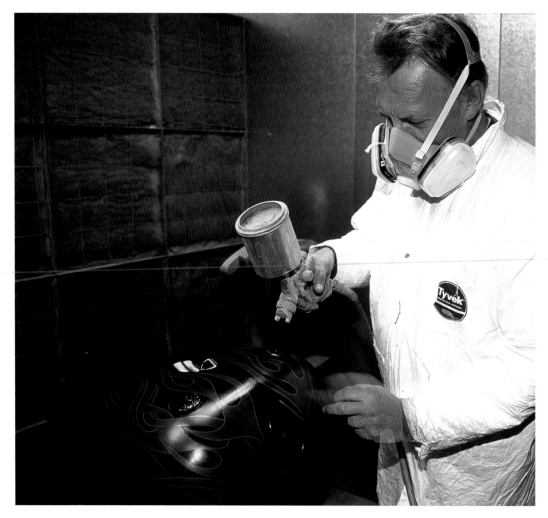

seventies, but they weren't as popular as they are now. I painted a few for the Hell's Angels back then, that's about the only people who had skulls on the sides of their tanks. The Death's Heads on their tanks are all different from each other, though basically they have the same layout, the Angels' logo.

'It's hard to say how long a job takes. They're all different and it's hard because I usually work on two or three bikes at the same time; while I wait for the paint to dry on one, I'll work on another one and jump back and forth, so it's hard to say – maybe a week on average? Sometimes I can spend a week just painting a mural. A week, and that's just the paint, not including any moulding, and the prep work takes a couple of weeks to get right.

'With the increased interest in paint jobs now I prefer to take on graphics-type artwork. So if I get people ringing up and they just want one or two colours, if I'm really busy, I turn 'em away. It's not so interesting. I've been working for Ron Simms for over twenty-five years. I take some other jobs from individuals but Ron is pretty much most of my work.

'I have a staff of two to help me. One guy does moulding for the frames and the prep work on the tanks and gets 'em ready to paint. Then the other guy, Mario, sprays the base colours and shoots the clear coats and does the polishing and touch-up work. One of the biggest problems I've had over the years is getting reliable people to do the prep work. It's really underestimated. It's kinda repetitious, so it's very hard to find someone who is willing to stay with it.'

DAVE HOSKINS

The bike ridden by Dave Hoskins of Swindon, England, is the realization of a 20-year-old dream to build and ride his own Harley chopper. Now in his 40s, and with three children, Dave's story is similar to that of many working-class men who operate out of their back-street workshops, scrimping and saving to buy parts and doing as much of the work themselves to save money. Not everyone has ambitions to be a master builder, appear on the Discovery channel and have a business operation turning over millions. Some merely long to own a great-looking chopper and ride it to their heart's content.

As was the case with a whole generation of chopper people in their 40s and 50s, it started with THAT film, *Easy Rider*. Dave was a kid when he saw it and promised himself a Harley chopper some day. For many, the dream faded as the day-to-day routine of work, mortgage, kids, etc. took precedence. Dave, however, managed to keep his dream going on a diet of custom-bike magazines, studying the choppers built by his heroes in the U.S.A. and Britain, and mentally constructing his own until time, money and circumstances allowed him to realize his ambitions.

Various bikes came and went over the years, including a Honda CB550 chopper, but they were mere substitutes for the ultimate chopper, and the option of buying an existing Harley didn't even enter his head, which would have been like riding someone else's bike. Dave's dream chopper had to be built with his own hands to make it truly his own.

OPPOSITE
Horst applies a coat of clear lacquer to a flame-covered fatbob tank.

LEFT
Dave Hoskins living the dream and cutting an imposing figure on the road with that extreme Wide Glide front end.

At last, in the late nineties, the time was right and he was ready to put his 20-year plan into action. As luck would have it, an independent Harley shop, Boothill Motorcycles near Oxford, had an aftermarket big-twin engine, a 95-ci (1560-cc) Sputhe to be exact. Dave bought the brand-new power plant and the heart of the chopper was decided. Dave wanted a chopper with exaggerated Wide Glide extended forks at the front and a big tyre at the rear. So, together with frame-builder Streetfighters of Leicester, England, a hardtail frame was constructed and it also made the horseshoe-shaped oil tank to fit the one-off frame. The forks were from a Kawasaki ZZ1100, extended by 10in (25cm), while huge slab yokes were made by JML and a ZZ750 front wheel with Kawasaki twin discs and calipers was fitted. The solid rear wheel was a one-off built by JML, which also supplied the forward controls. The rear wheel was shod with a 200 Avon, which is tiny by today's standards. The King sportster tank keeps the traditional chopper look going, but is modified with an aircraft-style filler cap.

In keeping with the traditional chopper theme, and to appear hard-core, Dave fitted a four-speed Rev Tech kicker transmission. Carbs were by S&S to feed the powerful Sputhe motor, while one-off exhausts were made by Dave of Planet Engineering. Dave did not want apehangers as the riding position would create too much wind resistance and fatigue. He intended to ride this performance chopper fast, so he fitted flat drag bars with an internal throttle mechanism. Paint was applied by Tombstone

Paint and of course featured flames, though Dave preferred an understated look so requested a subtle blue-flame effect.

Dave made his own seat, which was to have been solo, but when the kids protested, had to change it for a double. The chopper build has taken over two years to complete as Dave accumulated enough money to pay for all the parts. Many thought he would never

finish it, but with all those years spent dreaming, giving up was never an option.

Dave took the bike on its maiden voyage to the South West Custom and Classic Show, one of England's most prestigious events, and walked off with the accolade, Best in Show, which makes a very satisfying end to the story.

OPPOSITE
Dave has built a classic chopper for the modern era.

BELOW
A powerful Sputhe motor is at the heart of Dave's award-winning chopper.

Hot-rod artist Ed 'Big Daddy' Roth was a huge influence on Indian Larry, who used Roth's famous character, Rat Fink, on this gas tank.

INDIAN LARRY, 1949–2004

One of the most charismatic and individual men in the world of choppers, Indian Larry was tragically killed in August 2004 while performing his trademark stunt in front of 8,000 spectators at the Liquid Steel Motorcycle Show in Charlotte, North Carolina.

Larry Desmedt was well known to fans of *Iron Horse* magazine in which many of his choppers appeared. In 1987 it featured an Indian Chief chopper built by Larry, hence his nickname. At that time he operated out of a shop on the Lower East Side of New York called Psycho Cycles, which he shared with top leather-worker, Paul Cox. It was here in the mid-nineties that the author met and photographed Larry as he worked on a hot-rod Panhead he called the 'Bonneville Racer', which he later ran on the eponymous salt flats in Utah. We were introduced to one another by custom-bike journalist, English Don, who was also a contributor to *Iron Horse*.

Never judge a book by its cover is a saying that could well apply to Larry. To non-bikers he would have appeared intimidating, with his long hair, bandanna, tattooed arms and neck, heavy biker belt and biker boots, looking every inch the gang member. But Indian Larry never was; his left arm bears a tattoo which reads: 'No club Lone Wolf'. In other words he cut a path of his own in the world. Moreover, he was welcoming, friendly and delighted to receive a stranger in his shop.

Indian Larry was an honest man and quite open about his past; he had served time

in prison and was a recovering alcoholic. He was proud of the fact that he had cleaned up his act and was grateful that he was earning a crust doing what he loved best. I have seen many letters in the press written by people who encountered him while in the grip of their own demons and his sage advice and simple philosophy helped them turn the corner. At the time of our meeting he was unknown to the chopper world at large, *Iron Horse* being pretty much an underground magazine. The business card he gave me read: Indian Larry – Motorcycle Artist, Stuntman and Character. On the reverse was the legend 'No Guts No Glory'. That was in the nineties and for some reason the card has been in my wallet ever since.

Larry did have a taste of fame and

Indian Larry photographed at his Psycho Cycles workshop in New York's Lower East Side, where he was busy assembling a Panhead chopper.

fortune in the two years before he died, courtesy of the Discovery channel's *Biker Build-Off* shows, which made him a favourite with viewers and caused truckloads of his T-shirts and related memorabilia to sell at Sturgis, Daytona and Laconia. The mainstream of Harley bikers now regarded him as a star, and consistently placed Larry's choppers before more sophisticated and high-dollar creations.

Indian Larry's choppers were influenced by the style of the seventies: he was a great fan of Ed 'Big Daddy' Roth, to whom he dedicated a psychedelic gold metalflake Panhead by using Roth's famous character, Rat Fink, on the tank. Indian Larry's preference was for simple, very mechanical basic choppers with shorter springer front ends and he would challenge anyone to ride the back streets of New York on a long-forked rigid for any length of time. Larry's bikes were built to ride and he really liked to work them hard.

It was great that Indian Larry enjoyed some success before he died. He made his mark on the world of choppers and will be sorely missed. In later years he operated out of Brooklyn from a shop he called Gasoline Alley, hence the following:

> *And if I'm called away and it is my*
> *turn to go,*
> *Should the blood run cold in my veins,*
> *Just one favour I'll be asking of you,*
> *Don't bury me here it's too cold,*
> *Take me back; carry me back*
> *Down to Gasoline Alley where*
> *I started from.*

(Stewart/Wood).

OPPOSITE
Metalflake paint, Mustang-style tank and candy-twist front legs on the springers bring some seventies glamour to the 21st century.

LEFT
This bike is an eclectic mix that is 100 per cent Indian Larry. There is a Shovel front cylinder, a Pan rear fed by dual carbs, a dished gas tank and apehangers, and a high-tech inverted front suspension.

BELOW
This Swedish-style long bike was built by
Pat Kennedy for his wife Brooke.

OPPOSITE
Guardian of the tradition of the long
bike in the U.S.A., Pat Kennedy has
always followed the chopper code.

PAT KENNEDY

Pat Kennedy could be described as a biker-builder, the genuine article. The tattoos, beard, bandanna, and skull rings on his fingers, are not a cultivated image but a part of who he is. He was born into a biking family in California, having two older brothers who rode and built their own bikes. Consequently he has been working on them from an early age and riding them too.

Pat built his first bike, a BSA chopper, when he was 12. To him, choppers were cool and were all he wanted to ride and build – a principle to which he has remained true. While other builders follow changing fashions, he just kept on building long bikes from his shop in Oceanside, California, which he opened in 1979. Eventually, he realized he had had enough of California: there were too many people, too much pollution and too

much interference from the police. The last straw was when California passed a law making the wearing of helmets compulsory. Bikers were up in arms.

Pat decided to up sticks and move his business out to the historic desert town of Tombstone, Arizona, where he runs it from an old horse barn surrounded by high-security fences and cameras, which caused the locals to wonder what was going on. Had a ruthless

Brooke Kennedy may be petite, but she handles the long-forked chopper as well as any seasoned biker.

band of outlaws set up a clubhouse in their neighbourhood? Fears were allayed when it was realized that Pat and his partner, though bikers, were definitely not outlaws. Eventually, Pat and Brooke were married in Tombstone, they and their guests all wearing clothes from the days of the OK Corral.

Pat had been to Sweden, the land of the Viking longboats and, latterly, long bikes. The Swedes are crazy for low, long-forked choppers, which they build in communal workshops during the long, dark winters. Tolle is a Swedish company that produces extra-long hydraulic front ends and Pat

became an importer of its products, ironically returning the long-forked chopper to its country of origin.

During the nineties, therefore, while others were building billet barges and big baggers with lots of bodywork, Pat was working away in splendid isolation – a true

Pat's famous 'Alien' chopper is a futuristic vision which, with its faceted panels, resembles a stealth bomber. Does it evade police radar, perhaps?

Alien's bizarre and disturbing paint scheme was applied by Darrell Pinney.

guardian of the chopper ethic – preserving the secrets of rake and trail until the custom world returns to the true chopper way of thinking.

The silver chopper illustrated below and on the previous page is a bike Pat built for himself. His aim was to create something futuristic, with an alien, other-worldly appearance. Using a Kennedy chrome-molybdenum frame and a pair of 32-in (81.25-cm) over stock forks, Pat and his assistant, Ray Neff, fashioned a faceted, angular series of surfaces reminiscent of the

anti-radar bodywork of a stealth bomber, while Brooke – a specialist wheel-builder – took a set of eighties spoked wheels and laced them with diamond-cut spokes. The paintwork, executed by Pat's painter, Darrell Pinney, is a veritable masterpiece of skulls, drowning babies and weird extraterrestrial allusions, leading observers to remark, 'Man, what was that painter guy on?' The bike confirms, if indeed anyone doubted it, that choppers can be true art.

Brooke's chopper, pictured on page 292, is a maroon and silver creation, sporting 20-in (51-cm) over forks and a similar chrome-molybdenum frame which is stretched 10in (25cm) and raked to 45°. The swept-back handlebars are aluminium, as are the oil tank and forward controls and all have been anodized so that their colour matches the paintwork. Brooke laced up her 120-spoke wheels – a 19in (48.25cm) diameter front and 15in (38cm) at the rear. Darrell Pinney then applied a lustrous paint job which includes a complex scheme of skulls and graphics. Brooke is not a tall woman, but handles her long chopper with ease, a testament to the effectiveness of the geometry of stretch, rake and trail that Pat brings to his work.

Pat Kennedy Custom Motorcycles publishes a catalogue of Kennedy-designed and manufactured chopper parts, as well as the equipment it imports and distributes. Pat also builds bespoke bikes to order, but only a limited number every year. He only builds the kind of choppers he believes in and a good rapport between him and a prospective customer would have had to have existed before he makes a commitment. Only then

will he take a number of measurements, including height, weight, leg and reach of arm, much like a bespoke tailor in Savile Row. The scale drawings of the proposed bike are then prepared and varying paint schemes suggested. This was the approach taken when the editor of *Easyriders* magazine, Keith 'Bandit' Ball, brought his idea for a special bike to Pat for consideration.

The bike was to be built around Keith's vital statistics, being over 6ft (1.8m) tall and 220lb (100kg) in weight. It is a classic chopper which none of the newer West Coast builders has managed to better, though they have tried to emulate it. Pat's frame was high-necked and rigid, with a long springer front end with a chrome finish, and pointed a Brooke 21-in (53.3-cm) 80-spoke front wheel in the right direction, followed by an 18-in (46-cm) at the rear. The Evo engine was rebuilt by Lee Clement of Departure Bike Works of Richmond, Virginia, while the orange paint scheme, with its *Easyriders* logo, was applied by Darrell Pinney to a narrowed and lengthened Sportster tank and minimal hand-made rear fender. The bike was built for Sturgis 1992, a good ten years before many of the 'new' chopper shops had begun to re-invent the wheel.

Pat Kennedy is one of the most respected of the master builders and the builder of choice of many of the other big names. Choppers may have enjoyed a huge resurgence of popularity but, to bikers like Pat Kennedy, they never were a fashion statement – rather a way of life.

FRANK KOZIK

In the sixties and seventies in America, chopper riders seemed to come from fairly predictable backgrounds. They had predominantly working-class roots and were seeking a means of expression and an escape from a humdrum existence. They were typically mechanics, factory workers, construction workers or even plain dropouts, whose perceived lawlessness was perpetuated by the attitude of the establishment, which viewed anyone with a beard, long hair and tattoos with fear and distrust, making it more difficult for them to get employment.

Today things are very different, the advent of the Evolution power plant having civilized the Harley-Davidson. This fact, coupled with clever PR and marketing, has made the fantasy of the outlaw life attractive to a new range of affluent customers seeking release and excitement. It is because so many professional people like to live vicariously in their spare time that the popularity of the Harley is on the rise, the recent resurgence of chopped Harleys being the next logical step in the equation.

These days, it would be unwise to judge anyone riding a chopper by their appearance. Take Frank Kozik, for example. When he pulls up on his Shovelhead chopper and dismounts, stretches to his full height, long hair pulled back in a pony tail, with bushy black goatee beard and sleeves rolled up to show heavily tattooed forearms, it is easy to assume he is a One Percenter rather than a famous artist with work hanging in the Smithsonian Institution.

He first rose to prominence producing

Frank Kozik is an intense and philosophical man who likes to ride choppers. He is pictured here with some examples of his work.

Kozik, in his studio, reflects upon what chopper-riding means to him and is able to articulate what other bike-riders feel.

pop-art posters for up-and-coming rock bands in the U.S., while top names today, such as Soundgarden, Pearl Jam and the Red Hot Chili Peppers all had early promotional posters designed and created by Kozik. He is in fact a multimedia artist, having designed internet sites for David Lynch, created advertising campaigns for the likes of Nike, and has a cult clothing collection on sale in Japan.

So how does such a creative and highly-productive guy like Kozik get his kicks? He rides his Shovelhead chopper around the Californian countryside and through the quiet streets of San Francisco at 5 a.m. on cool summer mornings. A laid-back yet intense individual, Kozik describes what motorcycling in general and chopper-riding in particular means to him:

'You know, when you get on a motorcycle and you get really used to it, it tends to disappear and you can just sort of fly around? That's really the best part. To me

it's the equivalent of an orgasm or falling asleep; it's a pure physical experience because you have to be hyperaware, but at the same time you are hyperaware, you get so hyperaware that reality goes away. I've always lived in big cities, and I've always ridden in heavy city traffic, and I love it; it's like playing a video game every day. You have the manoeuvrability. It's just like the best thing ever, you know?

'I've always been a lone rider. The last couple of years I've gotten to know some friends here, though, and it's the first time I've ever gone out with a group of people on motorcycles. I usually hang out with other kinds of people, and for me the motorcycle is my escape.

'It's like once you're on the bike, the constraints of your reality disappear and, you know, I can be a World War 1 fighter pilot, I can go to the moon, whatever. That's the sort of thing it gives me, I love it. When I wake up in the morning I look forward to riding the motorcycle every day. I ride every day whether it's raining or whatever; in Texas I'd ride in snow, I didn't care. I crave it. The older I get the more I enjoy it. My riding skills have improved over the years, so it's like I'm being cut a finer and finer line.

'I also love archaic motorcycles. They're more of a challenge to ride, but I have a romantic notion of the past, and getting on an old bike sort of can transport me. So for me the motorcycle thing is personal: I don't go on runs, and I don't go to motorcycle events because I'm a fairly antisocial person. My motorcycles always have solo seats; I'm not interested in the passenger situation. To me

it's like a pure, a private experience, which is impossible for anybody to understand if they don't ride a motorcycle.

'I got my first Harley back in the late seventies. I had a car, and this guy wrecked my car, so he gave me his bike in payment. It was a piece-of-shit Sportster, a 1971, I think. It just was not a very well-made bike. I was kinda young and I didn't know how to manage a bike like that. That bike was a real hassle, so it kind of turned me off Harleys.

'Then about five years ago this friend of mine put together a bike, and he didn't like it. I had some money, and the price was right, so I'm like "Hell, I'll buy this Harley". It turned out to be the best bike I ever had.

'It's just a Shovelhead, a put-together Shovelhead, you know. Most of it is aftermarket rigid frame. When I bought it, he had these big fenders on it; it was all fifties-looking stuff. I've bobbed the hell out of it, but for some reason the engine has always been great. Every time I've worked on it, it runs better. I've totally fallen in love with this bike. It's the bike I have ridden the longest out of all of them, so after thirty years, I've found the right bike. I have money now, and I've been able to completely modify it to suit my every whim. It fits me perfectly. I don't even know if you can say it is a Harley, though. There's only about five per cent Harley parts on it. It's a Harley-influenced custom big twin.

'There's a mystique about a Harley-Davidson that's all tied into the power of America. Machismo and all that stuff, and that has an appeal too. When you roll up on a straight-pipe chopper, you do get a certain amount of respect from just about anybody that sees you. That's because when you're riding a chopper rigid, there's a level of awareness that you have to meet in order to successfully ride that sort of a bike. You have to literally ride the motorcycle, not just controlling the nicely balanced thing, it's like you have to figure out this bizarre combination of physical shit. With the chopper you learn to use the detrimental factors to your advantage for a different learning technique. It's like having a high-spirited horse under you.

'It's just nice to have this one-kind-of-a machine that you really know, I've done a lot of work on it, and friends of mine have done a lot of work on it, and it's kinda like a sculpture. I do spend an entire day just cleaning the bike. It's just completely satisfying, it's this perfect combination. It's beautiful to look at, it's fun to ride, it's cool to own, and it's the only one. It's my favourite thing, and I've had a lot of things in life. I could go out and spend a hundred grand on another bike, and it would never be the same. It has completely become an extension of my life.

'I live in San Francisco, which is a real pretty place, and sometimes I get up at five o'clock in the morning on a Sunday and I'll take off down the coast. My favourite ride is Highway 1 when the sun's coming up and it's not foggy and there's no traffic – it's paradise. I've ridden a lot of places, but I've never had the pleasure of riding that I've had in California. North of San Francisco there's this vast peninsula called Point Reyes, which is all forest. It's a beautifully preserved

landscape with these immaculate two-lane roads; on a weekday morning there's nobody up there. You won't see traffic for half-an-hour at a time, and there are all these beautiful small roads that wind through dairy farms. It's just amazing.

'Everyone has an iconic image of what a motorcycle is. To me now, that's a tough-looking chopper, a bobber. It looks aggressive, it's mechanical, powerful, and you want to ride it. I see some fancy bike; I don't want to ride it. It just comes down to that for me. To me performance is nothing. To me it's all like a visual appeal wrapped up with some romantic ideal. You know, that's what makes a motorcycle for me.'

Kozik's favourite bike, a hardtail Shovelhead chopper, taking shape in the workshops of California Choppers, San Francisco.

BELOW
The mural on Billy Lane's gas tank is a depiction of the very same bike heading off into the sunset.

OPPOSITE
Billy Lane arriving at the Biketoberfest *Biker Build-Off on his Knucklehead chopper.*

BILLY LANE

Born and bred in Miami, Florida, Billy Lane was interested in mechanical things from an early age. His father was into cars and hot rods in particular; consequently, this early exposure to custom cars and speed machines left an indelible mark and Billy eventually enrolled in engineering school. He now holds a science degree from Florida State University and a Bachelor of Science in Mechanical Engineering from Florida International University.

While still at college in 1989, he acquired his first bike. It was a practically useless 1950 Panhead but, with the help of a few old-timers, Billy managed to reassemble it and get it up and running. At that time it was unusual to see a teenager riding a Harley, let alone an old Panhead, which was thought to be the province of the old diehard greybeard biker.

Pretty soon, however, he was hanging out in clubhouses and drinking beer with patch-club bikers, the real hard-core element. These guys didn't believe in spending their money: if their scooters broke they stripped them down in their clubhouse and damned well fixed them. It is possible, therefore, that Billy learned more from them as to how a Harley is put together than in all his time at college. More important was the fact that he gained an insight into the character of old bikes which has a bearing on his work today.

Indeed, he is quite a philosopher when it comes to antique things. He appears to have an empathy with old inanimate objects, as if they had absorbed some of the spirit of the people who owned them over the years. He likes the patina of age on motorcycle parts, and the way an older engine's form follows function.

After college, Billy went to work in his brother's bike business, where he began to design special little parts for custom Harleys, in particular his 'six-gun' parts, which looked like a loaded six-gun chamber. These would appear on handlebar riser clamps, hand-shifter knobs, oil caps and footpegs. He realized that there was a market for these parts, which is what led him to form his own company, Choppers Inc., in 1995.

Billy began to build bikes in his own unique style, blending old and new parts to create an harmonious whole – a functioning piece of mechanical sculpture. Every bike he builds is unique: often he will include odd

ABOVE
Billy often uses odd pieces in his builds. Here he uses faucet handles on his springer forks.

ABOVE RIGHT
The hand-tooled leather solo seat looks like something Paul Cox would have made. Note the one-off oil tank with cooling fins.

OPPOSITE
Billy Lane enjoys the good life and the admiration that has come his way since the Discovery channel's Biker Build-Off *series made him a household name.*

objects, such as porcelain faucet handles marked hot and cold on the tap of a springer front end, or an art-crystal knob on a hand-shifter.

Choppers were not being built in 1995 by most of the master builders. Apart from Pat Kennedy, of Tombstone, Arizona, and a few others, no one saw a commercial market in long-forked bikes. This was soon to change, however, and Choppers Inc. saw itself well placed to take advantage of the resurgent interest in chopped motorcycles. Nowadays, it is impossible to walk ten yards down Beach St., Daytona, without seeing yet another bike business with the word chopper in its name. The bandwagon

has been truly boarded by all and sundry.

One of the reasons why the long chopper has become fashionable is possibly through the cable and satellite Discovery channel. It made a star of Jesse James of West Coast Choppers, and its subsequent series made household names of bike builders only previously known to Harley enthusiasts.

Billy Lane has become one of the most popular of the bike-building elite. Viewers respond to his image, that of surfer meets rock star meets biker, and find his down-to-earth approach attractive. Indeed at a Discovery channel *Biker Build-Off*, at Daytona Beach in 2004, packed crowds

waited for hours for Billy's arrival, surging forward to photograph their hero in a way that would not have happened in the past.

Billy himself seems to enjoy the adulation and is making the most of it, being a gregarious type who likes to chill out in the pool hall with an ice-cold Budweiser in his hand. He rides bikes every day and is happy to travel hundreds of miles to compete in *Biker Build-Offs*. If there is something called the 'chopper attitude', then Billy has it in abundance. A chopper is a statement, an in-the-face rejection of conventional society, an uncompromising ride. He rides his bikes hard and if he wrecks them he can always rebuild them.

Tig Leake proudly displays his 'Angelo' bike, a tribute to legendary biker/artist Dave Mann. It is as if Tig, a hard-core chopper rider, had stepped out of a Mann painting himself.

TIG LEAKE

Tig Leake is the embodiment of the outlaw biker in both appearance and attitude. Currently, he is not wearing colours, but he has in the past and will in the future. Tig took a long sabbatical from the One Percenter scene so that he could raise his son singlehanded. When his boy graduates, his

father expects to return to his old life.

He never quite abandoned the chopper scene, however. He is a petrolhead of the first order and owns a number of bikes, ranging from a classic Knucklehead of 1947 to a vintage Shovelhead chopper. In the bedroom of his house in Leesburg, Florida, a stock Panhead sits, which Tig bought for his son the

day he was born and will give to him the day he turns 18.

Tig began to ride choppers in the late sixties, but in 1971 a motorcycle magazine appeared that was like no other. *Easyriders* reflected the lifestyle of the American biker, giving an insight into the life of the 'scooter trash' biker, the parties, the runs, the women, the tattoos and, of course, the choppers. It provided a heady mix of bike features, jokes, cartoons and scantily-clad models (mostly amateur in the early days), which had never been done before.

On the centre spread of the third issue of *Easyriders* was an illustration by an unknown artist called Dave Mann, which was so powerful that an institution was born. Mann's art featured in each of *Easyriders*' centre spreads for the next 30 years and his vivid depiction of the lifestyle, of which he was a part, influenced generations of bikers. He painted the scooter trash biker in an heroic form, as the outlaw, the loner, the last American hero. Readers were quick to identify and soon Mann's centre spreads could be seen on workshop walls from Seattle to San Diego, Nova Scotia to New Orleans: he understood where they had come from and where they were going.

Tig Leake was a particular fan of Dave's work. In December 1973 *Easyriders* published one of Mann's illustrations of a red-and-yellow bobbed Panhead with apehanger bars, peanut tank, springer forks and a tall sissy bar. On the tank appeared the words 'Café Racer'. Seated side-saddle is a bearded and tattooed biker wearing a denim vest, while on the wall behind the bike are graffiti that read 'Know

ye that this is the kingdom of kicks – wine, bikes, drugs and chicks'. Beneath, it is inscribed, Angelo 3-12-58. Not surprisingly, this made an impression on Tig; he really dug the bike and told his friends he was going to build a replica of what they all referred to as the 'Angelo' bike.

Thirty years on and Tig began to fulfil his dream. He had been hampered in his task by the fact that, unusually, the Angelo bike was visible only from the left-hand side, Harleys most often being shown from the other side, where air filters and exhausts are visible. He knew what model of Harley it was – a Panhead – so was able to make an educated guess as to what the other side of the bike would look like. Clues such as the tips of the upswept pipes told him he needed a set of British-style 'trumpet' silencers.

These he managed to obtain, together with Knucklehead springers, chrome-tin primary cover, chrome Panhead coil cover, wide apes, high sissy bar and spoked wheels. He fitted Firestone tyres, a Bates solo seat and a Hydra Glide rear fender which he bobbed, while on the other side would more than likely have been an air filter from the Knucklehead era on a Linkert carburettor.

Dave Mann's attention to detail was legendary. On the Angelo bike, the rear fender has been bobbed (cut down); he even painted in the fastener holes which, on a dresser bike, would have accommodated the saddlebags.

Tig always wondered whether an actual bike and rider had been Mann's inspiration. Did the Angelo bike really exist? He decided

RIGHT

Having brought an imaginary bike to life,
Tig blasts his chopper along the highway.

BELOW

The peanut tank is painted exactly as it
was in the Dave Mann painting.

BELOW RIGHT

The clutch is disengaged by foot and
gears are selected by the most minimalist
of jockey hand-shifts

to write to Mann with the news that he was
building a replica, and asking whether the
bike was real or imagined, to which Dave
replied, thanking Tig for his interest, that it
had been a figment of his imagination.

This bike is a tribute of sorts. The 1963
Panhead motor was taken from a chop owned
by Tig's friend, Santa, who was sadly killed.
It is also a rolling tribute to the great biker/
artist, Dave Mann, who, since Tig finished
his bike, has sadly died.

HUGGY LEAVER

Londoner, Huggy Leaver, is a tough guy who hit the silver screen in a big way in the British gangster movie, *Lock, Stock and Two Smoking Barrels*, in which he realizes every city motorist's dream by abducting a traffic warden. While the film's director, Guy Ritchie, has moved on to the A-list circuit as Madonna's husband, Huggy is still working on and off in TV dramas and is currently appearing as a tough guy in one of Britain's soap operas, *Eastenders*, in which he more or less plays himself, sporting the classic fifties clothes that are his trademark.

In between acting jobs he sometimes works in a shop called American Classics, in London's King's Road, selling forties and fifties clothes. It should come as no surprise, therefore, that Huggy prefers an older style of motorcycle to propel him through the nightmare London traffic, his ride of choice being a 1939 74-ci (1200-cc) Model U Harley-Davidson, the flathead having been rebuilt in the true bobber style of the post-Second World War forties. In fact, a careful look at the background shots in Marlon Brando's film, *The Wild One*, will show that it is possible to see authentic period examples of Huggy's bike, which, with Huggy in his everyday fifties clothes of T-shirt, turned-up Levis and engineer boots, together recreate the fashions of the time in an uncannily realistic way.

There is a growing interest in bikes of this era in Europe, the U.S.A. and even more so in Japan. More and more are looking back to the era of the hot rod and bobber and building bikes which evoke those times. This

is not something Huggy is exploiting, however, as he has been riding flathead bobbers and looking this way since the early nineties. It is his way of life and will continue, even when the fashionistas have moved on to something else. Moreover, there are others, in and around London, who share his passions. They ride 45-ci (750-cc) Harley-Davidson flatheads, ex-Second World War U.S. Army bikes, which they have bobbed in much the same way as the returning servicemen in post-war California.

British actor, Huggy Leaver, is the epitome of fifties cool aboard his bobber.

Huggy's 1939 UL Harley has been bobbed using only period equipment that was available in the fifties.

Paul Bairstow, Huggy's good friend, is one of this group who can be seen frequenting the legendary ACE café in North London, while Paul's father, Tony, runs a business supplying all the spare parts and accessories that anyone could want to keep these 60-year-old bikes up and running.

There are a few guys riding 'flatties' around London who all know one another and get together for runs. A popular destination is the annual Old Timers' Rally in Den Haag, Holland, which only pre-1965 bikes are permitted to attend. This flattie crew all have an individual Vargas girl artwork on their gas tanks – a kind of group statement or talisman similar to that found on American bomber aircraft. Many of them also wear authentic leather flying jackets with either the original decals painted on the backs or replicas of them. It is thought that the outlaw motorcycle clubs' custom of wearing names and logos on the backs of their jackets (their club colours) stems from the way American bomber pilots also personalized their leathers.

Huggy has always ridden motorcycles and always preferred something basic and stripped-down in a street-scrambler or flat-track style. He has had his fair share of Triumph Bonnevilles and Tritons. In the early nineties he was riding a 1946 flathead Model U, finished off in black-and-orange. This UL bobber of Huggy's represents the earliest form of chopped motorcycle. Big-twin bikes of that era were designed for touring long distances across the U.S.A. They would have had screens, extra lights, saddlebags or panniers and the fenders would also have been large, made of heavy steel.

In those days bikers liked to attend amateur racing events and compete on the bikes they rode, and in order to achieve maximum performance they chopped off many of the extraneous parts. First to go was the whole of the front fender, while the rear fender was reduced so that it barely covered the rear wheel; lights were removed along with screens and bags. Sometimes footpegs replaced footboards and since much of the racing was on dirt track, longer springer front ends were fitted to improve ground clearance, the first instance of longer forks being fitted to stock motorcycles. Exhaust systems were cut back and silencers discarded, resulting in a rowdy, rip-roaring bike rather like the one Huggy rides now.

Huggy's UL was built over a period of six years as the parts needed were gradually acquired. By 2001, he had all he needed and he and Paul Bairstow assembled the bike in Huggy's kitchen, using only the authentic forties parts which would have

Huggy rides his flathead with casual confidence, carving his way through the nightmare that is London traffic today.

ABOVE

A Vargas girl adorns the gas tanks of all of Huggy's flathead friends. It is a lucky charm and echoes the kind of thing that adorned bomber aircraft during the Second World War.

RIGHT

The springers are from a thirties RL 45 Harley and are of forged metal rather than tubular.

been available at that time. Tony Bairstow also managed to find many of the parts and helped Huggy to rebuild the Linkert carburettor. The forks are springers taken from an early-thirties RL 45-ci bike, which were popular because they were of forged metal rather than tubular and were slightly longer than the stock springers.

Huggy is always planning new touches for his bike. He is thinking of putting VL springers on it, which are even longer, and will probably fit high-level shotgun pipes to make the bike seem more of a street scrambler. One thing is certain: Huggy will continue to cut a very individual dash through the red buses and black taxi cabs of London town.

THE MARTIN BROTHERS

Joe and Jason Martin are typical of the new wave of young bike-builders popping up all over the Unites States now that choppers are the new cool. Fifteen to 20 years ago the only people riding long-forked bikes with jockey shifts were dedicated lifetime bikers. Kids would see these grizzled, tattooed visions from another age and be too scared to catch their eye, let alone pluck up courage to inspect their rides or engage them in conversation.

Things are very different these days. Looking at the parade of bikes on Main Street, Daytona, one is struck by the number of Harleys that are high-dollar customs and by the fact that many are ridden by young kids, baseball caps back-to-front, wearing baggy hip hop-style clothes. Many would not be out of place at a Limp Bizkit concert. Indeed, lead singer Fred Durst rides Harleys, as does the other anti-hero, Kid Rock, who also includes members of the Outlaws motorcycle club in his videos.

Looking at the Martin brothers, one would guess they are in a band for sure, which would not be far from the truth. Before entering the bike scene, music was their

Joe Martin pilots his Biker Build-Off *project bike down Main Street, Daytona Beach.*

passion, but success and money were slow to come, consequently, they did a variety of jobs to keep body and soul together.

Significantly, Joe got a job in a garage which was frequented by the hot-rod fraternity, this being quite a scene in the Dallas-Fort Worth area where they lived. Here he learned the skills of a car painter and pinstriper, finding yet another outlet for his creative drive. Gradually, both the brothers became involved in customizing and decided to set up in business in the most rudimentary way possible. Their first paint shop was the kitchen of their rented house, which must surely have had a powerful extractor fan over the cooking stove!

Inevitably, someone heard about the brothers and asked if they would paint his bike, then the word spread and requests began to flow in. At first, because of lack of space, they found it easier to paint parts of bikes and were eventually able to provide the whole range of designs and murals. These were at their most extreme in custom Harleys and were probably more artistically challenging into the bargain. They also decided to buy a couple of old Harleys, a Panhead and Shovelhead, which gave them invaluable insight into the mechanical workings of big-twin motorcycles.

The boys recognized a purity of design in the chopper, where form can be more important than function. A chopper is challenging to ride, it has to be mastered and dominated by the rider, which goes some way to explain the chopper attitude and the disdain felt for the comfortable existence of mainstream society.

OPPOSITE
Who can doubt that building choppers is an art when confronted by this example of the Martin brothers' vision?

LEFT
Joe Martin fabricates his own frames and bodywork from scratch and is one of the few builders who applies his own paint.

OPPOSITE
The beautifully ornate hand gear-shift lever perfectly reflects the curves and lines of the frame and bodywork.

LEFT
One-off CNC-cut wheels reflect the 'tribal' design of the Martin Brothers' logo.

Chopper bikers want something different: in fact, a stock Harley-Davidson does nothing for them at all. Where the Martin brothers are concerned, each new custom build is a blank canvas waiting for an individual solution.

Joe is a hands-on builder, not a bike assembler, cherry-picking aftermarket parts from the shelf. He builds his own frames and fabricates bodywork and gas tanks out of sheet metal. His designs begin on a sheet of paper on which the overall silhouette of the bike is sketched. His style would seem to be influenced by the Celtic art and tribal designs popular in the tattooist's art. His is not a mere paint job; he actually fashions the shape of the bike part to reflect the way he is going to paint it, with a gas tank, an exhaust system or a swing-arm actually fabricated to accomodate the design.

The bike shown on these pages is Joe's latest *Biker Build-Off* project, its radical, spiky, other-worldly appearance being very much a Martin Brothers trademark. The boys are not in the business of mass-producing formula choppers, which they regard as contrary to the spirit of the chopper. However, they do design parts, such as exhaust systems, which they sell to other builders. Their custom bikes are works of art on wheels, helping to get them noticed and onto the all-important Discovery channel.

Martin Brothers has come a long way in a relatively short time, and is now based in Duncanville, Texas. The company employs around 16 people to build eight to ten one-off show bikes each year, and this in addition to all the parts they design, fabricate and sell. Check them out on Martinbrosbikes.com.

BELOW and OPPOSITE
Lawayne Matthies runs a company
called Mystery Designs. The chopper
trike here is its Torpedo model.

LAWAYNE MATTHIES

It was as natural as breathing that a young
farm boy, growing up in South Dakota,
should know how mechanical things came
apart and could be put together again,
especially as there was a 1937 Farmall
tractor which had to be kept up and running.
Lawayne, like many of his generation, owned
a number of muscle cars and was interested
in hot rods, so this stood him in good stead
when he began working on Harleys later on.

The big-bike rally at Sturgis was not far
from where he lived and it was over 30 years
ago that he first rode his bike there with his
buddies and has been to almost every Sturgis

ABOVE
The rear view shows the unique independent tilting suspension set-up.

ABOVE RIGHT
The Xzotic Panhead rocker covers on this twin-cam Harley motor were designed by Lawayne.

OPPOSITE
Lawayne demonstrates the unique tilting facility of the Tomahawk trike, the mechanism of which he designed together with a NASCAR engineer.

meeting since. Lawayne noticed, from the thousands of Harleys that gathered at Sturgis, even in the seventies (nowadays it is near 300,000), that it was necessary to build a crazy-looking bike in order to attract attention and stand out from the crowd. But the craziest thing he built in the late seventies wasn't a chopped Harley but a six-cylinder Honda CBX1000, which he had converted to a trike. It had no suspension, only wrinkle-walled drag-racing tyres on the rear two wheels. With a beast like this at his disposal, he was able to perform burnouts and crazy speed stunts to wow his peers and impress

them further by dodging the cops when they came to arrest him. Those were the wild days of Sturgis, when the bikers congregated in City Park; some of the stories of wild goings-on are unrepeatable.

Those were wild days indeed, and Lawayne was a rebel running free. In the late eighties, however, a combination of circumstances led him to take stock of his

life. He decided he needed something constructive to do and, bikes and bikers being what he knew best, set to work to build a business which he called Xzotic Motorcycle Products of Dallas, Texas.

Lawayne saw how Harley-Davidson exploited its long heritage – having been established since 1903 – by building new bikes with thirties-style springer front ends –

Springer Softails which, together with leather saddlebags, looked like old Knuckles and Panheads. The only thing that did not fit the equation was the modern-looking Evolution engine, but Lawayne saw that he would have a huge potential market if he could make it seem like an older Harley motor by making bolt-on parts.

To him, the Harley Panhead, in production from 1949 to 1965, was the best-looking of all, having featured in *Easy Rider* – a seminal film for a whole generation of Harley riders. He designed a Panhead rocker box-cover kit which replaced the stock Evo rocker box and transformed the look of the engine. He then designed old-style ribbed timing covers which bolted on in place of the stock item. Consequently, the 'Pan solution for Evolution' became his slogan, the products proving very popular. They were especially prized by other custom-bike builders, who used them on their show bikes.

The Xzotic product range, which Lawayne designed, gradually expanded until the day he received an offer he could not refuse and sold his company to Custom Chrome – an industrial giant which now markets his products. But one can't keep a good designer down and soon Lawayne was planning a new venture. He had noticed that there was a demand for Harley trikes and a number of companies were servicing that need. No one, in his opinion, had yet produced a good-looking trike conversion, those in existence being ugly 'truck trikes' which offended his designer's eye. As previously mentioned, he had already had practical experience in this field, having built

the CBX1000, and a Chevy-engined beast later on. He always felt that trikes had an inherent problem which made for poor handling, especially in the turns, where the rear wheels are dragged through the curve, quite unlike leaning a motorcycle into a turn. Lawayne felt that if he could make trikes handle more like bikes, the three-wheel experience would be transformed.

He set up a new company called Mystery Designs and began work to design and build a tilting trike.

The black chopper trike on pages 314 and 315 is known as the Torpedo model, while the blue-and-white is the Tomahawk, and have rear wheels taken from the Corvette. Note also the Xzotic pan covers on each motor. The two chopper trikes were launched at the Biketoberfest 2004 and caused quite a stir. Each was fitted with an ingenious NASCAR-engineered tilting mechanism with independent suspension, which enabled both rear wheels to tilt into the turns, improving high-speed cornering and rider feedback.

Mystery supplies the tilting suspension kit to other custom builders or it will build complete trikes to order. Chopper trikes are a revolutionary new development on the scene that not only look cool but also handle better than any other in production. As Lawayne says, 'We put the bike back into the trike.'

RUSSELL MITCHELL

Russell Mitchell runs Exile Cycles out of Sun Valley in the north Hollywood Hills near Los Angeles. However, he is an Englishman abroad, having come from very different hills near Gloucester, England. It was there in 1983–84 that he actually began to fashion two-wheel creations of a very different type from the fire-breathing hot-rod Harleys he builds today. Then, he customized Lambrettas – stylish little Italian scooters which had a cult following in Europe.

His first bike was Exile 1 and the second Exile 2. At this time Russell had no thoughts at all of emigrating, so the Exile Cycles were a happy accident, which became more relevant when he started up his Harley chopper shop near Los Angeles in the early nineties.

Russell won many trophies with his custom scooters, but was not allowed to enter them in Britain's premier show, which, at that time, was the Kent Custom Bike Show, run by the Hell's Angels Motorcycle Club,

OPPOSITE
The tilting ability of the Mystery trikes transforms handling and rider feedback, making the riding experience more akin to riding a bike which is leant into the turns.

BELOW LEFT
Russell Mitchell is an ex-pat Brit who runs Exile Cycles in the north Hollywood Hills in California.

her agency in Los Angeles. So off he went in pursuit of fame and fortune, which he found a few years later, not in the fashion scene but in the motorcycle fabrication business. Exile Cycles was born.

To understand the style of Exile Cycles' choppers, one needs to understand Russell. He has strong views on design, which were developed in Europe, influenced by Swedish and German minimalist styles. He is a bike-builder rather than an assembler of off-the-shelf parts. When he wants a component to look a certain way, he goes into his shop, starts up his lathe and makes it. His bikes are almost always painted black, with a satin or matt finish, and the brightwork is always stainless steel with a brushed finish, never chrome. He dispenses with everything apart

OPPOSITE
Russell calls his bike The Chopper as it represents the chopper bike in its purest form. The clean minimalist design is heavily influenced by the Swedish-style chopper look.

LEFT
Exile Cycles' best-selling part is this brake/sprocket kit where the brake caliper acts on the chain sprocket, thus dispensing with the need for a separate brake disc system.

BELOW
There are no levers, no cables and no compromises in Russell's quest for the ultra-clean look.

England. They had no wish to see these little 'sewing machines' side by side with the Triumphs, BSAs and Harley-Davidson choppers that made up the bulk of the show entries.

There was a lot of rivalry in sixties Britain between the BSA/Triumph-riding 'rockers' (bikers) and the scooter-riding 'mods', with their fancy clothes and attitudes, which led to a number of skirmishes in many a seaside holiday town

during the decade. It is likely that a number of Hell's Angels would have been involved in these fights, and were not ready to bury the hatchet 25 years later. So if Russell was to enter any of the big shows, he would have to start customizing 'real' motorcycles.

Russell was about to start work in London as a veterinarian when he met a girl working as a fashion model. He had done a bit of modelling himself to help himself through college, and she suggested he join

from what the bike needs to make it run. What is achieved is a clean, functional, 'tough' industrial look. His bikes reflect his own uncompromising attitude, which makes them far from easy to sell to Californians and Americans in general, who have been raised on a diet of gaudily-coloured bikes with an overemphasis on chrome.

The signs are that Russell is winning them over, now that he has been published in bike magazines all over the U.S.A. and Europe. He has appeared on Discovery channel's *World Biker Build-Off*, a highly successful series which commands a worldwide audience. His clients include Chris Cornell, former lead singer of Soundgarden, and Hollywood film actor, George Clooney, which has done much to raise his profile.

The bike shown here is modestly called The Chopper, and is pure Exile. Other than the motor and transmission, everything is manufactured in-house or distributed by Exile, such as the front ends, manufactured by SJP Engineering out of Holland. Russell also likes to use the Primo brand of external belt drive, which he considers to be the best available. As long as a part works and is tough enough to handle the high power outputs of his bikes, he sticks with them. This attitude ensures reliability, which equates with a good reputation in this market.

The Chopper has a 45° rake in the frame and a 4-inch (10-cm) upstretch in the front legs of the frame. There is an additional 6° of rake in the triple trees, making a total of 51°, which, combined with a 14-in (36-cm) over front end, gives the bike a good trail,

OPPOSITE
Russell tests all his bikes on the twisty roads of the Hollywood Hills. Here he appears to be keeping an eye out for the cops.

LEFT
The modern style is for increasingly fat back tyres. This 230 rear Avon fills Exile's Trojan rear fender, leaving just about enough room for tyre growth.

A 3-inch Primo belt drive transfers the power to the Total Performance motor to the clutch.

ensuring it handles well in the curves. The flat bars disguise the high neck of the frame, and combined with the positioning of the forward controls (footpegs), provide an extremely comfortable riding position.

To see Russell riding The Chopper in profile is to see what an integral part the rider is of the whole. This bike is a bespoke

creation, designed to fit Russell himself. He has created a Swedish-style chopper, clean and no-nonsense. The drag bars have no brake or clutch levers or any trailing cables to interfere with the clean lines. The throttle cable is routed inside the bars, and the left grip twists and operates the clutch via a pulley system in the transmission end which eases the load, making for a smooth operation.

The back wheel of the bike measures 15 x 8in (38 x 20cm) and wears a 230 Avon tyre running inside Exile's minimal Trojan fender. A close look at the rear wheel reveals Exile's *pièce de résistance* – its brake sprocket kit, a signature item, and its best-selling part. It dispenses with the need for a brake disc on one side and a sprocket on the other, creating more room for fat tyres and further simplifying the lines.

The motor is a 113-ci (1850-cc) Total Performance unit, strong and powerful. Total Performance build Exile's motors with an all-over aluminium-type finish, ensuring it blends with the stainless-steel parts. The motor exhales through a pair of monster 2-in (5-cm) drag pipes, while the transmission is a six-speed Jim's, driven by a Primo three-belt drive.

The bike is finished with satin-black paint on tank, fender and frame, while all the other parts in aluminium and stainless steel have a brushed, low-gloss industrial finish – which is the way Russell likes it.

ARLEN NESS

Now in his mid-sixties, Arlen Ness's creative flame still burns and he is the undisputed figurehead of the custom bike scene. He is a quiet, unassuming man, universally liked and respected. His hair and beard may now be white, but Arlen approaches his art with as much enthusiasm as he ever did in the San Francisco of the late sixties.

In the mid-sixties, Arlen was already married to Bev and working as a furniture remover by day and semi-professional bowls player by night. In 1967, however, when he was 28, he won a pot of money at bowls and went out and bought his first motorcycle, a 1947 Harley-Davidson Knucklehead, to which Bev responded that either the bike went or she would. Luckily for everyone

concerned, Arlen must have managed to talk her round or this important event in the history of custom bikes would never have developed. Bev and Arlen are still married and working together with daughter Sherri and son Cory at their new headquarters in the Bay Area of San Francisco.

Arlen took the old Knucklehead to pieces and added a peanut tank, giving the

In the sixties the grand master of custom bike-building, Arlen Ness, was instrumental in launching the then-new industry of aftermarket part production and distribution. Today, the aftermarket business for American V-twins is a billion-dollar industry.

bike a custom paint job himself. He had had some experience of modifying and painting cars, so the seeds of creativity had already been sown. They germinated when others were impressed enough to ask Arlen to paint bikes for them too. Arlen's new line of business flourished in the psychedelic sixties of San Francisco at a time that was

artistically creative – a revolutionary time of flower power, hippies, druggy poets – a happening time.

Arlen set up shop in San Leandro and, while his main concern was painting bikes, began to fabricate parts for them, including tanks, seats and handlebars, the Ramhorn style of which were his first commercial

successes. In the meantime, Arlen kept his day job, opening his shop only at evenings and weekends. But when he arrived at the shop to find a line of people waiting, he knew it was time to go for it in earnest.

He remodelled his Knucklehead and entered it in the Oakland Roadster Show, where it won Best of Show, indicating that

OPPOSITE
This, one of Arlen's most famous bikes, is 'Two Bad', a twin Sportster-engined low rider which is one of the most radical custom bikes ever made.

BELOW LEFT
Arlen pioneered the Bay Area Low Rider-style of chopper which was influenced by the long low drag-racing bikes. These were built for go as well as show and Arlen often installed superchargers to boost performance.

*The supercharger is driven by a belt
system powered directly from the
crankshaft. This ensures constantly
increased power throughout the rev
range.*

LEFT
Another blast from Arlen's past, the
'Untouchable', a supercharged
Knucklehead Bay Area Low Rider.

BELOW LEFT
In the late seventies and early eighties
scrollwork and the elaborate application
of gold leaf were popular, as was the
engraving of metal parts like these
Knucklehead rocker covers.

the hitherto unknown bike-builder had begun to establish a reputation. Thirty-odd years later and Arlen still has that same bike, which now resides in his new museum alongside almost 100 show bikes that he built for himself. These were never intended for sale, but some of them were theme bikes which went to corporate customers: in fact, he probably invented the themed custom bike.

In the early seventies he pioneered what became known as Bay Area Low Riders, with long, low frames, kicked-out front ends and swept-back handlebars. They were not choppers in the *Easy Rider* style but much more performance-orientated, like street drag bikes.

Arlen was one of the first to put two ironhead Sportster engines into one bike

RIGHT
The narrowness of the Bay Area Low
Rider contrasts greatly with the fat-tyred
choppers popular today.

FAR RIGHT
In the mid-nineties Arlen started the
fashion for 'taildraggers' where the all-
encompassing rear fender skims the road
surface, as is the case with this
Knucklehead chopper.

OPPOSITE
Arlen Ness was one of the first builders
to create theme bikes. This corporate
custom bike was built for the Avon tyre
company which regards the custom
Harley market as an important area of
its business.

Arlen loves to get out and ride whenever he can and can often be seen cruising the streets during Daytona Bikeweek.

frame, thus creating a radical beast. Many of his bikes featured superchargers, something he occasionally still does, even today. Even then, he was at the cutting edge, with many builders trying to emulate him but fighting to catch up. He has been constantly ahead of the competition, which is no mean feat. He was pushing back the boundaries of custom bike design while building a Knucklehead chop every year, at the same time creating a huge range of bolt-on accessories for the Harley-Davidson enthusiast. The advent of CNC machines and billet aluminium transformed his business, enabling him to produce his annually updated range of billet parts and accessories.

In the nineties, Arlen was at the forefront of designing what became known as 'luxury liners' – long, low, stretched bikes with all-enveloping bodywork reminiscent of cars of the thirties. This included the Ness 'convertible' – the futuristic yet thirties-looking 'SmoothNess'. He also designed custom baggers for the rider wishing to ride cross-country in custom style. Arlen himself rides up to Sturgis each year, often in the company of members of the Hamster club, which now numbers over 200 worldwide. While many of these bikes are the antithesis of the chopper, which should be a lean, mean stripped-down machine, this is not to say he had forgotten his roots. He has built choppers every year alongside what some people would call 'billet barges', while his Ferrari bike (see page 426) has appeared in art galleries around the world. If chopper building is art then Arlen is an old master.

When asked why he still builds bikes, Arlen responds that it is for the same reason he always did – for fun. Now that Arlen's son Cory, a great bike-builder in his own right, is taking care of Arlen Ness Enterprises, Arlen has plenty of time to enjoy riding his creations and having even more fun doing so.

Cory Ness is a talented bike-builder in his own right and now oversees the day-to-day running of Arlen Ness Enterprises.

OPPOSITE
This bike, built by Cory Ness, is called
'CurvaceousNess' for obvious reasons.
The bodywork is hand-beaten aluminium
rather than fibreglass.

LEFT
The headlamp fairing gives it an
aggressive sporting look.

PAGE 336
Cory built this gold-trimmed chopper in
a Biker Build-Off *against his father.*
Cory won, which suggests that the Ness
legacy is in good hands.

PAGE 337
The Teutuls, Paul Sr. and Paul Jr., are
TV stars, thanks to the reality TV series,
American Chopper. *Here they are*
enjoying a brief respite from the
thousands of autographs they sign each
day.

ORANGE COUNTY CHOPPERS

One of the most significant developments in the chopper scene in 2004–05 is the rise to fame of the Teutul family of Orange County, New York, builders of custom bikes. For the past couple of years they have been the subject of a reality TV show on the Discovery channel, which rivals MTV's *Osbournes* in terms of popularity with the public at large. Not everyone is a Black Sabbath fan who tunes into *The Osbournes*, neither is the huge majority that watch the Teutuls particularly interested in bikes.

Paul Teutul Sr. is a body-building giant of a man, with long walrus moustaches and a short temper, who storms around the shop, hurling insults at everyone in his path. His main victim is his son, Paul Jr., or Pauly, as he is generally known, who in spite of the abuse still manages to stay calm in the face of endless criticism. The verbal exchanges between the two usually culminate in Paul Sr. storming out and slamming every door on the way, and has to be seen to be believed. But it is plain to see that there is a tight-knit family, albeit with a unique way of relating to one another, beneath all the bellowing and bluster. Each programme takes the form of Pauly thinking up a theme for a chopper and inevitably facing tight deadlines, problems which are exacerbated by Paul Sr.'s tantrums. It manages to be funny and disturbing at the same time, while raising the profile of bikers and chopper riders in particular.

Paul Sr., who admits to a misspent youth involving drink and drugs, was nevertheless able to change his life around to create a successful company making garden fences.

OPPOSITE
This is a classic Knucklehead chopper,
from the dog-bone risers and sprung
solo seat to the upswept fishtail exhausts.
The black-painted rockers and timing
cover contrast well with the orange paint
job.

LEFT
A classic sixties Panhead chopper by
Orange County Choppers is proof that it
can build in the old-school style.

RIGHT and FAR RIGHT
This springer chopper displays all of the
traditional seventies chopper features,
albeit in an exaggerated form.

OPPOSITE
This extreme springer chopper is built to
fit the tall frame of Paul Teutul Sr.

But his son Paul graduated from college and was keen to put his engineering skills to work in a more challenging arena – that of building custom motorcycles. Consequently, they only became involved in bikes around 1999, so they are really the new kids on the block. Some criticize their work as meretricious in that it includes projects such as Jet bikes, Spider bikes, Fire Engine bikes, Lawn Mower bikes and so on. But the fact remains that if it were not for these unusual creations there would be no show, and children throughout America wouldn't be spending their pocket money on a range of toy replicas of their bikes.

RIGHT
The oil tank is adorned with a chrome likeness of Paul Sr., ensuring that it would not be wise to mess with this bike.

OPPOSITE
This bike, based on the theme of a U.S.A.F. fighter plane, is the kind associated with Orange County Choppers.

Whatever purists may think of their work, the Teutuls are a phenomenon of the bike world, with a gift of communication all their own. In their own way they are an example of the American Dream come true, in that they are the authors of their own success; the future of choppers seems to be firmly in their hands. It is also evident that the Teutuls are quite capable of building old-school choppers, in fact, a great deal of their business involves building choppers to order for their many customers.

When one sees them signing autographs at the Biketoberfest, for example, it is plain that the Teutuls' fans are from a broad spectrum, from leather-clad bikers to middle-class moms and their kids, prepared to wait for two hours or more to speak to their heroes. The barriers erected to control the crowd, which have become a necessity, are more reminiscent of a pop festival than anything seen at a bike rally before, yet Paul Sr., Pauly, brother Mikey and chief mechanic Vince, manage to handle everything with professionalism and grace. It is the best PR the chopper world has ever had and it is hoped that it may long continue.

MIKE PARTI

Mike Parti is a master restorer of vintage motorcycles, with the distinction of having worked on the collections of Steve McQueen and U.S. TV star Jay Leno.

He does not build choppers or ride them, but he appears in this book for a very good reason. He is a living, breathing link with the early days of motorcycle groups and the beginning of the custom motorcycle movement. Now 70, he grew up during the post-war period, when the returning Second World War veterans were starting up their motorcycle clubs and beginning to raise hell around California. At the time that the scandal of Hollister hit the news-stands, Mike would have been an impressionable youngster barely into his teens. By the time he was 15 he was already riding an old Indian around his neighbourhood, and at 21 had joined one of the toughest hard-core motorcycle gangs in California, the publicity-shunning 'Galloping Gooses'.

He has lost none of his toughness or his undying loyalty to his old club. He made no apologies for his actions in the fifties and sixties and doesn't intend to make any today. His club colours still hang on his workshop door, the central design being a fist giving the finger, decorated with the letters M and F – you work it out! At this point Mike will tell you some of his story, an authentic voice recalling the events and attitudes that have had far-reaching implications in the world of the chopper rider today.

'It's a funny story when I bought my first bike, that old Indian over there in 1950, aged 15; I was driving an old '34 Ford. I had an older friend, who lived in my neighbourhood, who was a mechanic for Glenbank Harley-Davidson. He was the guy on the block who welded up the kids' bicycles, an old drunk everybody felt sorry for. He was one of the Ghost Riders motorcycle club. One day I was over there and said, "Well I'll take my old Ford home and work on it; I got a leak in the radiator." He said to me "Mike, you know these motorcycles don't have radiators." I said "Yeah?" He said, "You don't have to crawl under them to work on 'em." I said "Yeah?" He said, "You know, Mike, with motorcycles, the girls are prettier." I became a motorcyclist on the spot – and I found that to be true, so he sold me the Indian.

'When I was a young man, I also was an outlaw, and I was in a club; it still exists, but I haven't been in it for thirty years or longer, called the Galloping Gooses. It was the heaviest-weight club at the time and met down in Los Angeles. I was in it eleven years, we had a lot of fun, raising hell, making a lot of noise. Mostly we drank beer, rode motorcycles and chased girls. We got girls round the back of the parked cars, that was a blast. The Gooses were a wild bunch, a real wild bunch and probably still are

'When I joined a few of the older ones were World War Two veterans. You had to be twenty-one to get in, which meant I was joining in about 1956. The guy who started the club was Dick Hershberg. They hung out in the Pullman, a bar right across from Union Station. Dick was sort of a loud guy, a real character, always making a lot of noise, always attracting a lot of attention. His bike was painted with a Galloping Goose symbol on the side of it. When I joined they were also hanging out down on Temple in Beverley, a place called the Caribou.

'They had their meetings in taverns and did a lot of riding, and some of them raced, like me. They were anti-AMA, and the AMA were anti us. They didn't like us because of our emblem, they didn't like us because of our attitude, and they mainly didn't like us because we were a pain in the ass. When I took up racing the AMA people used to make remarks about it – "Shouldn't wear those kinda colours on the racetrack" and all that. Well that's what I am: I don't apologize for who I am, and I don't apologize for my friends to this day. I've got friends on both sides of the fence. Very AMA and very other. I have a good time with all, but I know who my friends are.

'The club mostly rode Harleys. A few Indians, I rode a Moto Guzzi. So I was the oddball. We'd go some places and it wouldn't break down, so they began to grudgingly grow more respect for it. I rode Indian Chiefs, Indian Scouts, whatever the hell was runnin'. They rode VLs a little bit, but mostly Knuckleheads, a few ULs. The uniform of the day was different than today. We didn't allow any extra patches, and we wore Levis, sickle boots, T-shirts, club sweater and a leather jacket usually. We weren't into the long hair programme, although there were some people with long hair occasionally. The press thought it was a giant club, but it wasn't. We were limited to twenty-five members. We usually didn't have that many, just made a lot of noise, and they thought we were a lot more. All the kids did

was try to live up to the lies we told 'em, you know.

'We never did have any run-ins with other bike clubs. Mainly because they knew about us, and we had a few rules. One of 'em was you could not turn down a fight. You didn't have to win, but you had to go, and if you ran from a fight you were out of the club – your colours were pulled. I was one of the few people who retired with their colours. Because of the attitude of not running from fights ever, the word got around, and pretty soon people knew that if they were going to f*** with you, you were going to take them and have a fight, so they just made friends or left us alone, you know.

'We knew all the rest of the outlaw clubs, the Satan's Slaves and the Angels, and they were friends. We'd go visit them, they'd come visit us. The Angels were pretty good, but I though the Satans were really somethin'. These guys were really characters. The name of the game wasn't getting involved in criminal activity, just freaking out normal people and getting in the newspapers doin' somethin' crazy. Those guys were a thing all on their own, believe me, I still know a lot of them today.

'We were on the road most of the time. We'd get off work Friday night, head down to the taverns, and hang around there. Take off down to the beach. Start visiting other clubs, other bars and stuff, circle around, but I wouldn't go home 'til it was time to go to work on Monday. We'd sleep in ditches, we'd sleep under bridges, we'd sleep in parks – it wouldn't matter. There were various other clubs we'd go visit, or taverns

where there were groups of other motorcycle riders of our type. The bars were the Bungalow down in Compton, Janet and George's bar, and Blandy's in Culver City. Out here, Frenchies, and the Clubhouse, we'd just circle around the LA area pretty much. Later on some of the fellows took rides to San Francisco and places like that; go to Tijuana or whatever, just rides. Everybody hung together pretty good, somebody broke down, people'd wait on him. Sometimes we'd have a truck on a long trip in case something broke down, which you can count on most of the time.

'They were beautiful bikes, most of 'em painted black. I had a hand-shift '39 in '61, and the Moto Guzzi, and a Chief. A lot of 'em kept up to date and they had jockey-shifts, foot-shifts and all that, rather than hand-shifts. A few skinny bobs, but mostly fatbobs, fat tanks with narrower fenders, upsweeps, glides, high bars were very typical. The long-fork thing was after my time. I don't know why they started that, but I know why sissy bars came in. They passed a law saying you had to have a handhold for your passenger, so these guys just went burlesque with the thing and went apes*** building giant monuments on the back of their bikes. I never did that.

'We didn't call our bikes choppers. That came in later with the long forks, I think. We called them bob jobs. There was another kind of bob job of the era that we didn't have. At Long Beach there was a group that ran things called Long Beach cut-downs. They were older men than us. They were mostly VLs and two-cam JDs, which by the

way are quite fast. Small group – one of 'em was Wino Willie. I think Willie's still alive, if somebody hasn't killed him.

'The clubs I remember earlier, as I say the Gooses, Angels and Slaves, there was the Alameda Street Yellow Jackets, Boozefighters, the Moonshiners out of Compton, Cyclops out of Culver City, a Negro club called the Star Riders who rode the big full dressers, and they rode in formation about 90 miles an hour every place they went. A lot of chrome, a lot of stuff. Big club. They'd hang out at a bar called Sweet Dreams down on 44th and Central. I'd go down and visit them. Angels as far as I know started in '52 at Berdoo. The club I'm in now has a few of those guys in it, a club called Easy Riders, cars and bikes.

'I'm not in the Gooses anymore. I'm allowed to wear the colours, I've retired with my colours, but I very seldom do it. I'll tell you what it boils down to. If you wear those colours, you've gotta be able to take your place, you know, walk the walk. I'm not walking the walk anymore. It's bad for me to take credit for the guys who are walking the walk. I don't really represent them, I'll show 'em to you, my colours, no problem, but not to take pictures of 'em.

'The Gooses were a pretty wild-assed bunch in their day. I was at the AMA a while back and it was a club night, they were going to announce the names of all the old clubs, somehow the Galloping Gooses got in there on the list. You had to stand up and wave your hand if you were in the club. Their clubs, you know, they'd have a dozen guys there, when it got to the Galloping Gooses, I thought "Oh f***!" I got up and waved my hand high and sat down, and dead silence. Dingus Watson who is an old Goose was sitting there with me, and I said "What the f*** do you think of that?" He said "Well f*** everybody, they hated you when you were a kid." And they're sitting there that night, all these old men. Then

they all asked me "How come you guys were like you were?" And I said "you guys were just pissed off 'cause we got all the pretty girls. Usually yours!"

'One of the reasons I didn't ride Harley-Davidsons was on account of you took your Harley into a Harley shop, they wouldn't work on it. Other than a stock bike. I don't mean if you were an outlaw, but if you had

a bobbed up bike, they wouldn't take it. That pissed me off you know! I had nothing against the bike itself, per se, except the politics of some of the stuff they did. I get along with them fine today. In fact there's an artist coming to do some paintings of some of my bikes, they're going to hang them in some goddamn Harley Hall someplace.'

As one might expect, Mike has amassed a sizeable collection of memorabilia over the last 50 years, such as this ornate mirror presented to him to celebrate his status as master machinist and mechanic.

DAVE PEREWITZ

Dave Perewitz opened for business as Cycle Fabrications in Brockton, Massachusetts, back in 1975. The diametrical opposite of California, both geographically and climatically, it is no surprise that Perewitz developed an East-Coast style – slammed-to-the-ground FXR-based customs – all with variations on the flame theme applied by a master painter – Perewitz himself. People knew a Perewitz custom when they saw one: it had 'The Look'. Some say his bikes are all the same when actually each one is quite different, though all have that hard-to-define Perewitz style.

After 30 years of success in the world of custom bikes, Perewitz has seen it all, especially the resurgence of the chopped

motorcycle. Choppers are for kids, in his opinion, while older riders need a few more creature comforts. Choppers, however, make no compromises, they need to be dominated by the rider in the same way as a half-broken Mustang; unless you are bold and confident, it will turn round and bite you!

Perewitz builds bikes to sell and makes no apology for the fact that he runs a business to make money, so if there is a demand for the chopper style he is not going to ignore it. In his opinion a chopper has to be long, with a stretched high-necked frame, high-mounted tank and a long, raked-out front end, though some purists would say it has to be rigid. The rigid or hardtail look was adopted by early chopper-builders because it gave the best line and was simpler and cheaper to build. The softail-style frame mimics the line of a rigid chopper but allows a degree of suspension movement, thanks to a hidden shock absorber beneath the frame.

Ever mindful of his customer's needs, Perewitz has built a number of softail choppers but it is the slammed-to-the-ground performance look that is still associated with him. His skill with a paint spray is often not appreciated, his intricate, complicated flame designs being his trademark. The complex tracing and masking, spraying and pinstriping techniques, are a mystery to the uninitiated and a true art form. Not many master builders paint their own bikes, Ness used to, Joe Martin does, as does Dave, even though he claims he cannot draw.

Because he is undoubtedly an artist, he likes to build bikes, with the back-up of a fully-equipped machine shop, to his own template, dictating the lines and the way the components will flow together. His reputation is such that customers refrain from saying what they want: they just want a Perewitz bike, the like of which they have seen in countless magazine spreads. Dave can adapt the build of the bike to accommodate shorter- or taller-than-average customers – but that is it.

What with the way the custom scene is constantly changing, there is always something new to capture the imagination and Dave Perewitz, 30 years down the line, has not lost any of the enthusiasm that has given him a good living over the years.

OPPOSITE
LEFT
A huge bell-mouth on the carb sucks air into a Total Performance 124-ci (2000-cc) motor.

RIGHT
A single four-pot Performance Machine caliper and disc set-up provides the stopping power up-front.

LEFT
Perewitz is an accomplished painter who still works on many bikes each year. He is particularly famous for his intricate patterns of flames.

RIGHT
Peter Webber painted the classic
Marilyn Monroe Seven-Year-Itch *pose*
onto the stretched gas tank.

BELOW
This profile clearly shows the structure
of the extreme hardtail frame which
forms the skeleton of this chopper.

OPPOSITE
Mike Phillips is the head honcho of
Grandeur Cycle, a North Carolina
custom shop. He is one of the top East-
Coast chopper builders.

MIKE PHILLIPS

Mike Phillips, proprietor of Grandeur Cycle,
an establishment in Jonesville, North
Carolina, has been building bikes since he
was 13. A regular exhibitor at the Masters
Invitation custom show, Daytona Beach,
Mike is well known for the quality of the
work provided under the Grandeur name. He
builds a variety of styles, including beach
cruisers, luxury liners, baggers, pro-street
bikes and of course choppers.

The bikes selected here illustrate the two
extremes produced by Grandeur Cycle. The
long black bike represents the old-school
style of chopper. The extreme rigid frame
rises in swooping curves to an extremely
high headstock, which is raked and

accommodates a long, chromed springer front end. A four-pot brake caliper and disc on the front wheel is a safety compromise as a true old-schooler would not have had a front brake. Spoked wheels front and rear accentuate the traditional look, as do the whitewall tyres, while the absence of a front fender and a severely cut-back rear fender are pure chopper touches. It has an 88-ci (1450-cc) S&S Panhead motor, with period rocker covers and a ribbed timing cover that are identical to the Panhead that powered Wyatt and Billy's bikes in *Easy Rider*. The transmission is a five-speed Rev Tech with a primary belt drive, while the brass bicycle pedal kick-start is also a classic touch which is repeated on the foot controls for clutch and rear brake. Other touches of nostalgia are the cylindrical oil tank with 'mooneyes' and the 32 Ford stoplight with blue dot.

The short exhaust system has been routed around to the left-hand side of the bike, which is a neat touch. The only concession to comfort on this most extreme of choppers is the VTT suspension unit under the leather solo seat, designed to prevent kidney damage on rough road surfaces. The hand gear shift is an extravagantly-curved piece of chrome, the handle of which resembles the top of the springer forks. The short sissy bar completes the rear of the bike and is ornamental rather than functional as this bike is built for one. The tank mural, painted by Peter Webber, is a homage to Marilyn Monroe in one of her classic poses which, judging by the low seat and high tank, is all a shorter rider would see going in front of him.

OPPOSITE
The 'Marilyn' chopper is powered by a modern 88-ci Panhead motor made by S&S.

LEFT
This extreme chopper has a majestic appearance when viewed from a low angle.

RIGHT
This Penthouse, dragster-style pro-street
bike represents the other extreme of the
chopper scene, just as the Bay Area Low
Riders of the seventies were an antidote
to the long-forked choppers of their day.

OPPOSITE
This long, low, mean performance
machine by Grandeur Cycle utilizes a
Total Performance motor which has also
been turbocharged.

The Penthouse bike illustrates the other end of the chopper spectrum in that the only thing it has in common with the latter is that it is also a rigid. In the seventies there was a branch of chopper building that took its inspiration from the bikes of the drag strip. The Bay Area Low Riders had low, kicked-out front ends and large rear tyres, while Ness and Simms would often add a turbo or supercharger to further emphasize the fact that speed was a requirement of this style of bike.

The modern pro-street look is very much in the same mould but updated to accommodate the high-tech equipment used in the V-twin drag-racing world today. This is a tarmac-tearing hooligan of a bike, its monster turbocharger mounted to the right-hand side of the engine. Its rotors are spun by the exhaust gases which pressurize the air fed to the TP motor, giving a huge increase in power. Anyone riding this had better hold tight, for when that turbo engages and that huge 300 Avon grips, the bike launches itself like a bat out of hell.

BELOW
Top British chopper-builder, Phil Piper, surveys his latest handiwork, the show-winning 'Yo Daddeo'.

RIGHT
The three-spoke wheels are a one-off designed by Phil and thanks to an Exile brake/sprocket unit on the left side can be fully appreciated.

PHIL PIPER

Phil Piper is a purist where choppers are concerned in that he believes they should be rigid or nothing. After 20 years of building some of the best choppers to have emerged from the British Isles, Phil must have made quite a saving by not buying any rear suspension units. Operating out of Leicester, England, as Phil's Chopper Shack, he has built a reputation as a top builder and designer of an increasingly wide range of clever Chopper Shack parts.

Back Street Heroes (*BSH*) magazine is the largest-selling custom-bike magazine in the U.K. and has existed for over 20 years, about the same amount of time that Phil has been building choppers. It is fair to say that he has had more bikes featured on the cover of *BSH* than anyone else; this is not to say that the number of bikes he builds is high,

but rather that their quality automatically causes a stir. Each year Phil builds one bike for himself and another for his partner, Debbie, and may also take on three or four other commissions for private customers.

He has customized many makes, including BSAs, Motor Morinis and Triumphs, but it is the Harley-style big twin that is the focus of his work. Each of his choppers is an individual work of art and each is given a suitable name: Shovel Trouble, Shovel Trouble ll, Flame Job, Devilution, Pandemonium, Ghetto-Blaster, and lately, 777. These bikes are well-known

PAGE 359
The orange metalflake paint on this chopper harks back to the seventies. Phil Piper is a purist and believes that a proper chopper must have a rigid rear end.

OPPOSITE
Phil built this Sportster-based chopper which he calls 'Hotrod' for his partner, Debbie.

LEFT
This bike is called 'Pandemonium', a play on words, as Phil has fitted Xzotic Pan rocker covers to the motor.

RIGHT
This is the bike known as 'Devilution'.

OPPOSITE
Bikers who have lived with Shovelhead Harleys smile wryly at the title of this chopper – 'Shovel Trouble 2'.

show choppers, having won on many occasions, as the bulging trophy cabinets in Phil's house confirm. One would no more adapt or change any of these bikes than paint over a Van Gogh.

Phil takes his influences from the hot-rod car culture, Ed 'Big Daddy' Roth, and Von Dutch, and particularly admires the work of Lou Falcigno of C&L Hogshop, Florida. He

also rates the work of Jesse James of West Coast Choppers as well as that of fellow Brit, Russell Mitchell, of Exile Cycles, California.

Phil's latest creation, the satin-black chopper he calls 'Yo Daddeo', is thought by many to be his best to date. Completed in 2004 it won Best in Show at the Rock and Blues custom show, considered by many to be the most important in the U.K. The impetus for this bike came when Phil made his annual trip to California, where he always attends Jesse James' 'No Love' ride.

Calling in to see Russell Mitchell of Exile Cycles, he spied a most desirable-looking V-twin motor sitting on the workshop bench, which turned out to be a Total Performance 124-ci (2000-cc) unit delivering 126 'kick-ass horses' straight out of the crate. Moreover, the package came complete with a 45-mm Mikuni carburettor and a Crane ignition kit. When Phil heard that Russell had used more than a dozen TP motors without problem he put in an order on the spot.

With the motor safely back in the U.K. and sitting on the workbench, Phil considered the next phase. A show-winning chopper will always need tricky-looking wheels so Phil set about designing the pattern he wanted, deciding upon a 21-in (53-cm) front and 18-in (46-cm) rear. He also decided on a three-spoke design reminiscent of the twin-bolts-of-lightning design popular with the One Percenters, leaving it to CNC specialist, Mick Davies, who duly turned the design into a reality.

The frame is a one-off single-downtubed drilled-out rigid designed by Phil and fashioned by Classic & Custom, while the forks and yokes are Fat Glide 12-in (30.5-cm) overs by SJP. He decided, in pursuit of an old-school look, that the frame should have no panelling or plating at all, rejecting any tab-type brackets so that all fixing points were turned or cut and threaded on the lathe before being welded to the frame.

The gas tank is a stretched Sportster item which has a subtle swage-line around it; the rear fender also has a couple of swage lines to complement the gas tank, which was achieved with the help of a specialist in sheet metalworking, John Lister. A Tolle pop-up filter cap was installed into the tank and a recessed Dakota digital speedo was also fitted.

The solo seat was hammered out of 2-mm mild steel sheet over a curbed dolly. The seat cover was made by Outback Motorcycle Saddles and features Western-style cross-whipped stitching, the leather engraved with the letters FTW and a Maltese cross. The two-into-two snake-eyes exhaust system was handmade by expert pipe-bender Phooey in North Wales. It had always been intended that the bike should be finished in satin-black and the hot-rod look was further enhanced by the addition of period artwork by Vince Ray.

The TP motor was mated to a Rev Tech six-speed transmission and primary, while the chain final drive turns on a clever Exile Cycles brake/sprocket combination kit, where the inboard calipers act on the sprocket and dispense with the need for a disc brake system. This leaves the right side of the rear wheels 'clean', so that the one-off

wheel design by Phil can be fully appreciated. The bike is trimmed with Chopper Shack Maltese cross-decorated axle covers, risers, air cleaner and mirror. The Maltese-cross number plate/stoplight assembly is also from Chopper Shack and has no external wires, while Exile Cycles supplied the beefy-looking forward controls.

Phil has created a street-tough, hot-rod of a chopper, with an aggressive riding position and tree-pulling power. The triple sevens on the tank finally indicate that Phil has hit the jackpot and he has the show wins and trophies to prove it.

OPPOSITE
The silhouettes of these two bikes, built by Phil Piper of Chopper Shack, look very different in the setting sun. On the left, Debbie's Sportster has a long-wheelbased rigid frame but retains a reasonably stock-looking front end, while on the right the classic long-forked chopper lines of Phil's bike are shown to advantage.

REDNECK ENGINEERING

Just when everyone is asking how far choppers can go, someone goes there, this radical praying-mantis-style creation by Redneck Engineering of Liberty, South Carolina, being just such an example.

Redneck Engineering offers a number of models based around various frames of its own design and fabrication, and won the title Frame Designer of the Year at the 2004 Cincinnati V-Twin Expo.

This new breed, referred to as 'curve choppers' by some, 'radial hoppers' by others, have an appearance that is futuristic yet with echoes of the past in the swoops and curves of the frame tubes and handlebars. The balloon-tyred beach-cruiser bicycles of fifties America, by Schwinn, have had an influence on the design of this bike, called 'Chrome Curves', by Redneck Engineering,

and similar designs seem to have simultaneously emerged from Independent Cycles, Goldhammer, Jesse Rooke and Top Shelf Customs; traces of the old board-track racers can also be detected in many of these. Chrome Curves has a number of interesting

features. When viewed from the side, one is struck by the amount of space there is between the bike's components. There does not seem to be enough there to enable the bike to run, but it does. The oil tank is cleverly hidden and is an integral part of the

lower rear fender. The fuel is held in the swooping gas tank, which is totally hand-formed by Redneck, and all cables are hidden within the handlebars and frame tubes to keep the lines uncluttered.

The chromed frame is raked out to 42°,

Redneck built this racy-looking bike around a Sportster motor, achieving a look which is known as 'streetfighter' in Europe.

This extended springer chop by Redneck is powered by an S&S Panhead motor and, as is the fashion, is pushed along by an extreme fat rear end.

while the 12-in (30.5-cm) over front end is a Mean Street made by Redneck, as are the handlebars which are called Redneck curves. The 21-in (53-cm) front wheel is by Weld, bears the design of a spider's web and wears a Metzeler tyre. At the rear, an 18-in (46-cm)

Weld wheel is shod with a big 280 Metzeler tyre. The rear sprocket and brake are part of an integral system supplied by Exile Cycles and modified by Redneck, while the seat height must be about as low as it can go without dragging one's rear on the asphalt.

The engine is an S&S 124-ci (2000-cc) Kendall Johnson-assembled unit mated to a Roadmax transmission and a BDL 3-in (8-cm) primary belt drive. The slash-cut swooping exhausts are by Wicked Brothers.

Redneck's other curve chopper is painted

black and called the Ugly Bike. It has retro touches such as a lengthened springer front end and a Panhead motor by S&S. The retro parts are offset by very modern three-spoke billet wheels by Weld.

Vince, Redneck Engineering's chief, enjoys seeing these new ideas transferred from the drawing board and taking shape in the workshop. He is from the Carolinas and a slogan is emblazoned on the back of his

truck. It reads, 'We don't give a damn how they do it on the West Coast'. Now Vince, tell me that wasn't you in the pickup truck at the end of *Easy Rider*!

This radical framed chopper is ironically called the 'Ugly Bike'. Note how the rider sits within the bike due to the extremely low seat height.

JESSE ROOKE

Jesse Rooke is one of the latest of the 'Young Turks' invading the chopper scene, having built his first custom bike in 2002 when he established Rooke Customs. Still in his 20s, Jesse had an engineering background as he once had a business in Phoenix building 125-cc racing karts for Kawasaki and also raced his own framed Kawasaki-powered karts to success in world championship events. He had also been involved in

motocross until a serious accident when he was 15 left him paralyzed and unable to walk for three years. But Jesse overcame his injuries and managed to regain the use of his legs.

In January 2002 he had another life-changing experience. He had sold his business, MPH Inc., and was intending to race karts full-time, when he happened upon a show on the Discovery channel featuring Jesse James of West Coast Choppers and

was inspired enough to give custom-building a go.

Six months later he had built Dinah (most of his creations eventually received girls' names), which he entered in the LA Calendar Show 2002, a hotly-contested popular West-Coast event in which he won the ultimate prize – Best in Show – an unprecedented achievement for one so young and barely six months into a new career. Following this, he featured in Discovery's

ABOVE
The front suspension is based on a Schwinn bicycle design which dates from 1938 when Jesse's father had not even been born.

OPPOSITE
Even though this Rooke custom bike does not have too radical a front end, it still has a style identifiable with the young Jesse Rooke.

Motorcycle Mania and Speedvision's *American Thunder*, and to cap it all made the cover of *Hot Bike*, one of America's premier custom-bike magazines. Jesse was now in the big time, as far as the chopper scene was concerned; the question was – could he keep it up?

In January 2003 Jesse built Phyllis, his next creation, also referred to as the 'Last-Century Chopper'. This was a build-off challenge to Jesse James, where they each

had to produce something fast and aggressive before riding them out together. Phyllis was featured on the cover of *Street Chopper* magazine, leaving the chopper community in no doubt that a new challenger had emerged, and who deserved be taken seriously.

Next came Cathy, built in 27 days as part of Discovery channel's *Biker Build-Off*, which in 2003 also won the LA Calendar Show. Cathy is Jesse Rooke's signature style

which he calls a Kalikruiser and features his tricky single-sided rigid rear-wheel assembly. It also features a Rooke custom single-sided front-fork suspension called Nanna. The inspiration for the bike is the 1938 Schwinn bicycle cruiser with its distinctive swooping lines. This style was exploited even further in his next show-winning creation entitled Chopshop, on which he recreates Frank W. Schwinn's 1938 cantilevered front-fork suspension.

While Cathy is powered by a new 2003 Indian Power Plus 100, Chopshop has an S&S 124-ci (2000-cc) unit built by Kendall Johnson. The Mikuni carb is supplied with gas, not from a frame-mounted gas tank because it hasn't got one. The gas reservoir is inside what conventionally would be the oil tank, concealed within the rear rigid single side arm and decorated with the number 27 (the number of days it took to build the bike). A Baker right-side-drive six-speed transmission and a Baker clutch transmit the engine's awesome power to the rear PM casino wheel via a Baker primary and chain final drive.

Chopshop is an extraordinary piece of art and engineering with many one-off parts fabricated by Jesse. The castellated top clamp on the front headstock, and similarly fashioned jockey shift, reflect Rooke Custom's logo, the rook chesspiece, as does the sprung solo seat made by Jesse. It would be a shame to use this bike, which should go straight into an art gallery. Once again, Chopshop took the LA Calendar Show, giving Jesse a hat trick of wins. Hats off to a new young master builder.

BELOW RIGHT
Bay Area veteran Ron Simms is pictured
here in his new showroom, a converted
furniture warehouse near San Francisco.

OPPOSITE
All Simms' bikes have a tough street look
and astonishing paint schemes, courtesy
of master painter Horst.

RON SIMMS

Big Ron Simms of Hartford, near Oakland, San Francisco, is one of the Bay Area veteran bike-builders with over 30 years in the chopper business. In the sixties the Bay Area was seen as a 'Garden of Eden', a place where many significant cultures and movements evolved.

The psychedelic movement of Ken Kesey and his merry pranksters, the student anti-Vietnam War movement of Berkeley College, the Black Panthers, Sonny Barger's Oakland chapter of the Hell's Angels, were all rocking to the throbbing beat of the Grateful Dead, Jefferson Airplane and the Doors. Against this backdrop motorcycle artists such as Arlen Ness, Barry Cooney, Denver's Choppers and Ron Simms were

OPPOSITE
Ron Simms built his bike for the Camel
Roadshow which travels to all the big
bike gatherings around the U.S.A.

expressing themselves through radical custom Harleys which became synonymous with the area, i.e. the Bay Area Low Rider style. Often utilizing the ironhead Sportster engine, the low riders were, of course, low to the ground, with spindly-looking frame tubes, springer or girder front ends and ornate finishes involving intricate engraving of the engine casings and cycle parts as well as gold-plating. Paint jobs were suitably psychedelic and often included superb applications of gold leaf. Painters such as Horst and Jeff McCann were the pioneers of motorcycle paint jobs, while the Oakland Roadster Show was the most prestigious event for the hot-rod crowd and the motorcycle fraternity was soon to be included.

Ron Simms grew up in this milieu: he was used to seeing the Hell's Angels running in packs through the neighbourhood and regarded them as cool, seeing them as the last American outlaws, blazing a trail of their own and cocking a snoot at authority wherever they encountered it. The Bay Area was and is a tough neighbourhood and young Ron Simms was a tough kid. Long before Jesse James discovered 'attitude', Simms already had it by the bucket-load and had the 'gangsta' thing going long before Kid Rock ever cut a track.

Ron Simms' Bay Area Custom Cycle (BACC) came into being in 1973 at a time when just about everybody was customizing Sportsters which, due to their integral engine and gearbox, were easier to graft into frames. They also gave better performance than the old Panheads and early Shovels.

The guys in 'The Club' (Hell's Angels are always referred to as members of *The* Club), had their own chopper style in which small

Sportster or little Mustang scooter tanks were put into big-twin rigs, mounting them high on the frame tube. This became known as 'Frisco'-style.

In the late sixties the Bay Area was a hotbed of street and drag racing and a few people were beginning to build low, light-framed bikes with stroked Sportster engines and big back tyres. They looked like drag bikes on the street and were called 'diggers' or in some quarters Bay Area Low Riders. These were featured in magazines such as *Street Chopper* or *Big Bike* and the style quickly spread to other parts of the U.S.A. Ron believes that the custom bikes were called 'street diggers' because of their power, which they manifested by digging or tearing up the asphalt. These bikes would be lavishly decorated with elaborate paint jobs and had their engine casings engraved, although Ron did not care for that style too much. He claims that BACC was making billet parts about ten years before anyone else.

Simms' style of custom bike is instantly recognizable and can be summed up in one word – TOUGH! They are huge, big-inch thugs of motors which he helped to develop – powerful, chunky-looking monsters that scream bad attitude. The paint jobs often reflect the 'gangsta' look with illustrations of skeletons armed with machine guns making a regular appearance. Skulls and flames are a staple of the custom paint scene but Simms' paint jobs are far removed from the average fare. This is because he works with another denizen of the sixties Bay Area, a reclusive publicity-shy individual by the name of Horst (see page 280). In the opinion of Simms and

many others, Horst is the best there is, and Simms refuses to use anyone else if he can help it. Horst specializes in an oddball juxtaposition of colours that should not work but does. He also achieves an amazing quality of depth, applying layer upon layer of paint until one seems to be looking through a forest of flames to a scene beyond in a truly three-dimensional effect. Simms believes they were exponents of the tribal designs before anyone else and that the broken marbled effect was also used by BACC 15 years ago.

Ron still likes to throw a leg over a bike and take off whenever business commitments allow. It is part of his personality that he likes to ride hard and push on. He is averse to riding in groups that waste time and stop at every opportunity. It could be said that 'he doesn't play well with others', like the T-shirt says. While he feels the chopper revival has been good for business, he also regrets the erosion of individuality.

At a Long Beach show he attended, 80 out of the 120 bikes present were choppers with the same frames, the same gas tanks and the same pipes. But Ron has no intention of switching to pure choppers while people still want his tough thug bikes, but he will turn out the occasional one just to show what his shop can do. He is also encouraged by the huge interest among the younger generation for custom bikes. He gets a lot of customers in their 20s coming through his showroom and they are buying bikes, and if they don't there are always Simms' biker clothes, designed to make them look cool out on the street.

RIGHT
*This bike is called 'Simply the Best',
which says a lot for the confidence of the
builder.*

OPPOSITE
*Erik Vauth, of the German House of
Thunder, put an untold number of hours
into this bike and in doing so set new
standards in the world of custom bike-
building.*

SIMPLY THE BEST

The bike modestly called 'Simply the Best'
was built by the German, Erik Vauth, who
together with his brother Jörg runs House of
Thunder in northern Germany, where they
are regularly to be seen on the drag strip.
They like to build performance rubber-
burning custom bikes and consider it good
PR for clients to see their bikes put through
their paces, seeing it as a mark of
confidence in the standard and reliability of
their work.

Erik and Jörg prefer to build extreme
custom bikes from the ground up rather then
modify stock Harleys. They were once
approached by a customer with a simple
requirement: he wanted them to build him a
bike that would win shows at Daytona
Bikeweek. He wanted it to be reliable,
rideable and street-legal on U.S. roads, which
is how they came to build a clean, stylish and
ground-breaking custom bike that would
cross new technical frontiers. Simply the
Best is a mind-blowing combination of
technical ingenuity and artful metal
sculpture. Arlen Ness was present when the
bike was unveiled at Daytona Beach 2002,
where he was seen to shake his head
incredulously, muttering, 'Man, this raises
the bar to a new level for everyone.' Praise
indeed from the Grand Master.

The bike is ultra-clean and free of clutter,
the handlebars having no levers for clutch or
brake and the footpegs no pedals for
gearshift or braking. The clutch is hidden in
the left-hand handlebar and is operated by a
twist grip that activates an hydraulic cylinder,
while the right-hand grip operates the throttle

RIGHT
Ultra-clean bars are free of levers and cables. The left handlebar is a twist-grip clutch, while the right is a conventional twist-grip throttle.

BELOW RIGHT
Spark plugs and leads are cleverly disguised and hidden.

BELOW FAR RIGHT
The balance and symmetry of the metalwork and graphics are a tribute to the ingenuity of the builder.

OPPOSITE
Simply the Best set a new standard when it was unveiled at Daytona Beach in 2002, a truly ground-breaking vision of perfection. Many builders have since risen to the challenge posed by House of Thunder.

in a conventional manner. Braking is by two heel-operated levers behind each footpeg, which operate a high-tech aluminium-ceramic pulley brake system. The front brake calipers are integrated into the lower legs of the font forks which are made by Goldhammer.

Technology usually to be found in the world of Formula One racing is used for shifting gear and is achieved by push-buttons on the handlebar which operate magnetically. The frame and bodywork is hand-made throughout by House of Thunder, whose list of parts and modifications is almost endless, while the engine is largely from a stock 88-ci (1442-cc) Harley-Davidson. It is not known how many hours this creation devoured, only that it took a long time. Virtually everything visible is from House of Thunder, down to the painted graphics and their application.

When photographed, Simply the Best was a running, functioning motorcycle, a true example of rolling art from the land of Porsche and Mercedes.

BELOW RIGHT

Donnie Smith was building girder fork choppers the first time around more than 30 years ago. Here we are in the 21st century and it is déjà vu all over again.

OPPOSITE

The girder forks may be of seventies vintage but the rest of the bike is pure 21st-century chopper: softail frame, billet wheels and huge rear tyre.

DONNIE SMITH

Donnie Smith is considered to be a member of the older elite among chopper-builders, along with Ness, Perewitz and Fatland, but it doesn't mean he is ready to throw in the towel just yet.

A look at the detail on the blue Shooting Star chopper, illustrated here, and one can see how the blend of old-school touches with modern technology has created a chopper with classic lines that is more user-friendly than those of the seventies. At first glance it appears to be a rigid, but a closer look reveals that it has a softail-style frame, which affords the rider a degree of kidney protection in the suspension movement. A low yet comfortable padded solo seat indicates that it is intended for distance riding rather than flitting from bar to bar. The chromed girder front end is a throwback to the seventies when Donnie began constructing the choppers that were to make him one of the master builders and an early member of the yellow T-shirted elite, the Hamsters, members of which are still friends and with whom he rides the Black Hills near Sturgis to this day.

As with most of his bikes, Shooting Star is powered by a big-inch TP motor, while a tricky down-draft carb supplies the oxygen and a pair of 2-in (5-cm) upswept shotgun pipes gets rid of the exhaust. A huge rear boot of a tyre ensures the look is up to date and is wrapped in a cutaway rear fender which is moulded to the swing-arm. Another old-school touch is the omission of a front

The 124-ci Total Performance V-twin power unit seems to be a favourite of many of the top customizers.

builders, who had a better and earlier introduction to machines and combustion engines as a result. On a farm one has to fix things oneself and an understanding of all things mechanical comes with the territory.

Early experiences on a Triumph in the mid-sixties gave Donnie an appetite for riding but it was not until he returned from his tour of duty for Uncle Sam in 1970 that he set up in business with his brother. The film *Easy Rider* had fuelled his interest in choppers, and people now wanted to look cool on a long bike. This included Donnie's uncle, who asked him to rake his motorcycle frame, which Donnie proceeded to cut up and weld back together again. Often, in those days, a longer front end would simply be added, with the result that the bike did not sit right, giving it a sit-up-and-beg appearance. The two bikes in *Easy Rider* had been properly custom-built with stretched frames and raked headstocks, which kept them long but with the bottom frame tubes parallel to the road, which looked great.

When bikers saw that Donnie could make something they could not, they offered him the dollars and Donnie Smith's career path was no longer in doubt. He has featured in the *Biker Build-Off* series, where he demonstrated his ability to walk the walk with the best of them out there. He still likes to pound out the miles, whenever his busy schedule allows, relishing the feeling of being in his own private bubble, a stress-relieving Zen kind of state which most bikers would recognize.

fender, which could be a problem when riding in the rain; however, the high-necked frame and wide tank probably prevent spray from drenching the rider.

Donnie has been turning out bikes from his shop in Minnesota since 1971. He refers to himself as a farm boy, which is no different from many of the other top

ROBERT & HARLEY SMITH

Father and son double act, Robert and Harley Smith, make an interesting study. Robert, also known as 'Dark Star', is a custom-bike painter, and can look back over 30 years of chopper riding and building. He is unquestionably of the *Easy Rider* generation, in that the film characters played by Peter Fonda and Dennis Hopper were instrumental in forming his ideas. His son Harley, however, represents the new wave of riders sweeping America, influenced by the West-Coast chopper style pioneered by Jesse James and many others who came later. Harley, aged 23, differs from many of the

There are different eras and different generations, but that same old chopper experience keeps coming around.

New-school, old-school: father and son, Robert and Harley Smith, love to hit the highway on their choppers. So much for the generation gap.

new generation in that what he saw on the TV Discovery channel was not his primary influence but was inherited from his 'old man'. Harley was literally born into the chopper lifestyle and intends to uphold that legacy in the aptly-named Bloodline Choppers, a bike-building business that is still in its infancy.

Theirs are the authentic voices of the back-street builders, their choppers being their only asset in that they are built with their own bare hands. Not many kids of Harley's generation can claim to have built their own chopper from the ground up and painted it while still barely 20 years old.

Robert's life on two wheels began in the sixties, on a series of Cushman scooters, before progressing to Triumphs. The movie *Easy Rider* was released in America in 1969 and, like *The Wild One* of 1953, left a whole new bike culture in its wake. Swept along on the tide of its influence, Robert acquired a Harley Sportster in 1970, with a 15-in (38-cm) over front end, but with no rake in the frame so that it sat up high at the front, which was typical of the time. It was an easy matter for anyone with a little mechanical knowledge to extend the telescopic forks and stick them back on before adding some apehanger handlebars and a sissy bar.

In 1971 Robert transferred his Sportster engine and transmission into a hardtail frame, adding a springer front end. He also fitted Invader wheels and his life in choppers truly began. In those days, specialist chopper shops and painters were few and far between and people did far more themselves, so it was natural that Robert should paint the bike

himself. He made a good job of it and news of his talent spread far and wide. Thus did Robert realize that he could leave the factory and make a living doing what he loved best.

In 1980, Dark Star Custom Paint was established in Dallas, Texas, the name of the business and eventually Robert's nickname having been taken from a favourite love song by Crosby, Stills & Nash. This was also the name of his first chopper, which he always keeps in his bedroom wherever he lives.

A few years later he acquired a 1951 Panhead Harley which was mildly chopped. This he put into a Denver hardtail frame with a 12-in (30.5-cm) over front end, and continued to ride it for the next ten years

Robert, also known as Dark Star, has incorporated many old-school touches, such as the fork gaiters, dual seat and narrow rear tyre. He based the build on one of the last genuine Denver's Choppers' frames.

Harley Smith's bike is based on a Gambler rigid sport classic with a 200 rear tyre, which is modest by today's standard.

until financial difficulties, a wife and a new baby forced him to hock it for cash. This was hard to bear in that he was painting choppers every day but without a bike of his own.

The bike on page 389 came into being after years of scrimping, saving, bartering and stashing away of parts until he was able to start building it. In 1993 Denver Mullins, of Denver's Choppers, sadly died, and Dark Star wondered if any frames had survived. They had – a softail and a rigid. Of course Robert took the rigid frame and was able to build the chopper he had always wanted.

The Denver hardtail frame has a 2-in (5-cm) stretch in the front and a 33° neck rake, the adjustable triple trees from Germany giving it a total 51° of rake. The forks are 16in (41cm) over with 6-in (15.25-cm) risers, the bars taken from a Heritage-model Harley which have been bent in a vice to the required shape. The rubber gaiters of the fork are Harley-made and add an old-school touch. Robert opted for a stock Harley motor, transmission and primary for reliability's sake, due to the fact that he puts high mileage on his rides. The engine is rubber-mounted in the frame, having the effect of reducing vibration, and for more old-school cool, Xzotic Panhead-style rocker covers designed by Lawayne Matthies of Dallas were added. The blue-and-yellow metallic flame paint job (no other would do) finishes off the bike, and that is how it is going to stay.

In 1998, the year of Harley's graduation, Robert decided to give his son his first chopper, so that they could make a cross-

Harley has created a chopper that has classic lines. He was inspired by Jesse James of West Coast Choppers, who has communicated the chopper ethic to a whole new generation.

country ride together, their destination being Sturgis. However, the story is complicated, involving deals, debts and favours, but the bike that Harley ultimately received was an authentic old-school Sportster chopper hardtail, with 20-in (51-cm) over forks with no front brake, as was the style in the

seventies. It was not the ideal learner bike in that it handled like 'a barrow-load of wet cement' in the curves. But common sense prevailed and they loaded the choppers onto a van. Harley therefore learned his craft in a baptism of fire, riding up and down Spearfish Canyon in the Black Hills of South Dakota.

He rode the Sportster for two years until, one rainy night in Dallas, he was cut up by an inconsiderate car driver and fell badly, damaging the bike. However, the subsequent insurance payment provided the funds for the first chopper the built himself. He used the money to buy as many bike parts as

The 80-spoke rear wheel fits snugly in a modified Jesse James fender. The flame paint job was applied by young Harley himself.

possible, ignoring such mundane things as food and rent.

What Harley wanted was a proper hardtail chopper and decided upon one built by Gambler in Tennessee, a Rigid Sport Classic. It is a high-necked style with 2in (5cm) of stretch in the backbone and 4 in the downtubes. It is raked at 43°, intended for a 12-in (30.5-cm) over front end. He also wanted a little more length in the forks and

fitted a raked-out set of triple trees to stretch the bike out further. The risers are by Choppers Inc. of Melbourne, Florida, with the distinctive six-gun bullet-chamber top clamps and are 8in (20.5cm) long. Flat bars bring the grips to shoulder height, creating a comfortable arms-straight-out-in-front position.

The front brake is stock Harley, while the rear is from Performance Machine. The

rear fender is a Diablo from Jesse James, which he managed to obtain at the right price. It was not wide enough for a 200 rear tyre, so he cut it in half and welded a strip of metal in to make it fit. The fuel tank is a 1996 Sportster model, which was the year capacity was increased. Harley modified the mounts, welding a petcock into the bottom corner so that all the gas (petrol) was made available. There is no reserve: when the tank runs out it really is empty.

The 21-in (53.5-cm) front wheel is stock, shod with an Avon Road Runner, covered by a Jesse James fender. The rear is an aftermarket 80-spoke tubeless wheel, shod with a 200 Avon. The motor and transmission are stock 1999 80-ci (1300-cc), chosen as much for price as reliability. Forward controls are by RC Components, designed so that pegs, shifter and brake levers are all on the same axis, which is expensive but looks clean. The oil tank is a modified Harley Softail, while ignition is a Harley aftermarket Screaming Eagle. Exhaust pipes are 2-in Kromewerks shotguns, while the Maltese-cross tail light adds a touch of old-style chopper.

Being the son of a painter, there was nothing for it but for Harley to spray his chopper himself, using a House of Kolor Candy-Apple Red over a silver base, with flames in Tangerine Candy over a silver base. Lastly, a classic Bates headlamp was added to light his way home from his job as a bar-tender in Dallas. The work of both father and son seems to encapsulate the idea, 'The way we were, the way we are and the way we are going to be'.

EDDIE TROTTA

Eddie Trotta's career has been a varied and interesting one. Not many people have managed to run with a pack of wild One Percenters while working for a degree at a famous school of music. Eddie managed to practise his piano and still find time to mess around with his brother's Knucklehead chopper. Indeed, when Eddie was barely 13 in the mid-sixties, he was helping to rake and stretch the Knucklehead to radical proportions, well before anyone had seen *Easy Rider*.

Eddie built his own Shovelhead chopper when he was 16, while working for East Coast Choppers in New Haven, since when he has remained addicted to the long chopper, where the rider sits in the chopper rather than on it and becomes almost an integral part of the bike, which is what Eddie likes to see.

Pat Kennedy is a builder whom Eddie admires, who in the early nineties was importing Tolle forks and adjustable triple trees from Sweden, the land of the long nights and even longer choppers. The Swedes knew the formula for calculating the degree of rake and the requisite amount of stretch to create a perfect steering geometry and a bike that handled well. This made the long chopper a great deal less daunting to ride and opened up the market for them as a result.

Among his other talents, before he became besotted with choppers, Eddie had been a professional gambler and race-horse owner in Florida. He had also had success in the dangerous sport of power-boat racing, evidence that he was living in the fast lane,

At one time, Eddie Trotta was set on a career as a concert pianist but circumstances dictated that his hands would play a different tune in the world of chopped Harleys.

OPPOSITE
Eddie built this bike for the Seminole Hard Rock Hotel & Casino display at Biketoberfest Daytona 2004, which is fitting since Eddie was once a professional gambler.

LEFT
A Thunder Cycle motor by H&L is the power unit of choice.

BELOW RIGHT
Eddie achieves a seamless union of
fender and frame, finished off with an
exotic solo seat covered in alligator skin.

OPPOSITE
This silver ghost-flame chopper
incorporates a single side swing-arm
with inboard brake disc.

taking chances and running free. But Eddie fell ill for a time which rekindled his early interest and led to the establishment of Thunder Cycle Designs in Fort Lauderdale, Florida, supplying high-dollar custom motorcycles to famous stars of sport and screen.

The silver chopper illustrated opposite is a typical example of a Trotta hi-tech custom,

notable in particular for the tricky single side swing-arm, right-hand belt drive and inboard brake disc. A long upside-down front end and a stretched frame create a classic chopper profile, while the gas tank is stretched and flows into the moulded bodywork of the rear fender assembly.

The slash-cut, upswept drag pipes create exactly the right lines to complement those

of the frame and the silver metallic paint with subtle ghost flames creates a classy finish. Another subtle touch is the way the three-spoke pattern of the wheels is also reflected in the pulley on the rear wheel. It is this attention to detail and economy of line that elevates a chopper such as this from good to great.

CHAPTER EIGHT
ON THE ROAD

The act of riding a motorcycle has long been romanticized and invested with an almost metaphysical quality. The union of man and machine and the lure of the open road has been much eulogized, even to the point of cliché. But when it comes to riding a Harley-Davidson it becomes even more than that. The Harley is one of America's iconic symbols. It appeals to the pioneering spirit in that it is the ultimate freedom machine, able to transport its rider in more ways than one.

In a mysterious way it can almost be regarded as a time machine, in that the frontier days of the Old West seem to be replicated in it. Harley riders subconsciously identify with the image of the 'lone rider', alone in the wilderness with only his trusty steed for company, and even more parallels can be drawn in the leather vests and chaps, the conchos on belts and saddlebags, the fringed jackets, tooled leather saddles and Western-style boots, sometimes even worn with spurs. The black biker T-shirts often bear images of lone wolves, soaring eagles, Native Americans in heroic poses and other images of a wilder more natural environment.

There is the romantic notion that the lone

rider is outside the law: he is a nomad, always on the move and free from family ties. The notion of the 'good' outlaw is a popular one, with many examples in history.

There is the semi-legendary Robin Hood who, together with his 'merry' men, once roamed Sherwood Forest in England, robbing the rich to give to the poor. Then there are

the James brothers, Jesse and Frank who, together with the Youngers, robbed banks and railroad barons whom they considered to be cheating the ordinary folk out of land and

OPPOSITE
FAR LEFT
Welsh chopper rider Dick Tree reaches for his jockey-shift and changes gear.

TOP RIGHT
Bjorn, a Hell's Angel, rides a rigid-framed Harley with Evo motor and Swedish Tolle forks.

BELOW RIGHT
Women are an increasingly common sight in the world of custom Harleys.

LEFT
Harley Smith rides the chopper he built and painted himself in true Jesse James style through Florida's Everglades.

RIGHT and FAR RIGHT
Apehanger bars seem to bring a
superior kind of 'chopper attitude' to the
rider.

OPPOSITE
Two members of the Harley Owners
Group enjoy a blast through the
lavender-scented countryside of southern
France.

money. Billy the Kid, Butch Cassidy and
Sundance, Bonnie and Clyde, John Dillinger
– all command a sneaking respect, despite
being outlaws, and have been romanticized in
Hollywood films.

Many of the outlaws were nomads,
displaced by catastrophic events such as the
American Civil War, the Great Depression of
the 1930s or the Second World War. Indeed,
many of the outlaw motorcycle clubs were
started by war veterans, displaced and

OPPOSITE
Terry Sweeney pilots his Knucklehead chopper through the fields of southern England.

LEFT
A member of the Outlaws MC powers his way through a curve. He is in England, which explains why he is on the left-hand side of the road!

Chris Brown's rigid Shovelhead utilizes a springer softail front end and handles well in the curves.

traumatized by their experiences and alienated from normal society.

Often, these 'trouble-makers' on motorcycles are feared and reviled by ordinary citizens and vilified by the press. It could be said that the motorcycle outlaw was a creation of the media, fed by the oxygen of notoriety and eventual glorification in film.

The film, *The Wild One*, presented Marlon Brando as Johnny, a vulnerable, inarticulate disturbed youth, who nevertheless is able to spark feelings of sympathy within the audience, which concluded that it wasn't all his fault.

It is often said that 'every woman loves an outlaw' and probably believes she can

reform thim: it could also be said that 'every man would like to be an outlaw', if only for a day. In a scene from the film, *The Loveless*, starring Willem Dafoe and Robert Gordon, a garage proprietor, is observing the antics of the young motorcycle hoodlums repairing a Harley in his workshop. He turns to his son and says to him longingly, 'Hell, what

LEFT
'Prof' demonstrates that his old 45-ci (737-cc) flathead is just as cool as any big-inch chopper costing thousands of dollars more.

PAGE 408
Martin Henderson, of Boothill Motorcycles, U.K., pilots his bobbed rigid Panhead through country lanes.

PAGE 409
An unknown rider arrives in Red River, New Mexico, on a raked ironhead Sportster.

wouldn't I give to trade places with them for a day.'

Hunter S. Thompson, an American writer, spent a year hanging out with the Hell's Angels in San Francisco in 1965, which led to his seminal book, *Hell's Angels: the Strange and Terrible Saga of the Outlaw Motorcycle Gangs,* in which he remarks that the motorcycle outlaws: '… are acting out the daydreams of millions … who don't wear any defiant insignia and who don't know how to be outlaws. The streets of every city are thronged with men who would pay all the money they could get their hands on to be transformed – even for a day – into hairy, hard-fisted brutes who walk over cops, extort free drinks from terrified bar tenders and then thunder out of town on big motorcycles after raping the banker's daughter. Even people who think the Angels should all be put to sleep find it easy to identify with them. They command a fascination, however reluctant …'

Even the outlaw's regalia and insignia have entered the psyche of those who dream of freedom, who imagine themselves riding a huge Harley and disappearing with it into the sunset. The Harley-Davidson Motorcycle Company, which for years disassociated itself from the Harley-riding One Percenters, eventually realized that it could capitalize on this more exciting outlaw image. Moreover, the Harley Owners Group (HOG) is structured to reflect the organization of a trade union while retaining the raffish image. It is divided into regional 'chapters' and has 'officers' who proclaim their membership in the form of backpatches sewn onto leather

jackets or vests. Cleverly, Harley-Davidson has managed to convince ordinary law-abiding citizens that they too can experience the life of an outlaw, if only vicariously, by buying one of its bikes.

The westward migration of the pioneers in their wagon trains, pushing back the frontiers of the continent while facing hostile tribes, is where it all began. The gold rushes that drew thousands to California, the Black Hills of South Dakota and the Klondyke all demonstrate the willingness of early settlers to venture out in search of a better life, while the Great Depression of the 1930s led many thousands to pile their belongings onto an old Model T Ford and head west to California. These migrants settled in places like Oakland, San Francisco, and it was their children more often than not who ended up forming the first outlaw motorbike clubs.

Americans are jealous of their right to

OPPOSITE
Solo seats on choppers may look cool but the advantages of a dual seat should not be underestimated.

BELOW LEFT
Ian Borrowman hauls ass on his extreme Swedish-style chopper.

OPPOSITE
Alan is Black Bear Harley-Davidson's
parts manager (U.K.), so after a
scratched Ness headlamp unit was
discarded it was miraculously
reincarnated on his hard-core chopper.

LEFT
Blue skies, sun, sea, sand and a
Knucklehead chopper ... How cool can it
get?

*The image of the lone rider as an heroic
nomad is an enduring one.*

roam, searching for the freedom that is the open road, the endless ribbon that makes them fire up their muscle car or Harley-Davidson and take off for horizons new. As Willem Dafoe soliloquizes in the introduction to the film, *The Loveless*, '...this endless blacktop is my sweet eternity'.

Riding a chopper revives these feelings in the ultimate outlaw ride. The chopper is a machine that refuses to conform to the stock factory way of doing things. A chopper should be an individual that stands out in a crowd, a long-forked hardtail with bad attitude that, in a perfect world, mirrors the character of the man who built and rides it. On such a bike, the outlaw is saying, 'I ain't going to be no man's friend today.'

This is 'chopper attitude', summed up perfectly on the first page of Hunter

ABOVE LEFT

No longer can anyone associate the chopper rider with the scooter trash image of the past as the younger generation moves in with their hip-hop baggy look.

ABOVE

Butch's Shovelhead is making rapid progress.

LEFT

This chopper is called 'Meltdown' and was built by Sooty's Customs, England.

RIGHT
Denny Lueder and partner ride their
Shovel chop from their home in Omaha,
Nebraska, to Sturgis. The small leather
saddlebags mean they must be selective
packers.

OPPOSITE
Choppers like these are a very common
sight today. Their rise in popularity has
seen an influx of 'new' riders, who do
not conform to the biker image in any
way.

Top British chopper builder, Phil Piper,
riding his chopper, Pandemonium.

Thompson's book as he describes the ultimate motorcycle outlaws out on a club run near San Francisco in the summer of 1965: '…running fast and loud on the early morning freeway, low in the saddle, nobody smiles, jamming crazy through traffic and ninety miles an hour down the center strip, missing by inches …Like Genghis Khan on an iron horse …Tense for the action, long hair in the wind, beards and bandannas flapping, earrings, armpits, chain whips, swastikas and stripped-down Harleys flashing chrome as traffic on 101 moves over, nervous, to let the formation pass like a burst of dirty thunder …'

That thunderous sound of a big V-twin engine beating down through shotgun pipes is also an essential ingredient in the mix which contributes to the chopper-riding experience. Roll back that twistgrip, clutch in, snick up a gear and open up the throttle again as the beast roars and accelerates, the asphalt a blur inches away, leaning into a turn and powering through, eager for the next one, the smell of the countryside rushing by and the warmth of the sun, no deadlines to make, the destination being only the ride itself.

You don't have to be an outlaw to enjoy the experience and dreaming is not yet illegal, so as the bikers' anthem, *Born to be Wild*, dictates:
Get your motor running … Head out on the Highway.
It doesn't matter what you're coming from,
It's where you're headed that counts.

This rider looks to be hauling ass as he speeds along Boulder Canyon towards Deadwood, South Dakota.

RIGHT
A hard-core biker blasts from stoplight to stoplight in a blur of tank and body art.

OPPOSITE
Committed chopper riders, Logie (left) and Charlie (right), think nothing of jumping on their hardtails in Scotland and blasting down to the South of France or Spain for a weekend partying.

CHAPTER NINE
THE ART OF THE HARLEY

The year 1998 was significant in the world of motorcycles in general and Harley-Davidson in particular, when the Guggenheim Museum in New York mounted an exhibition entitled, *The Art of the Motorcycle*, which traced the evolution of the motorcycle over the last 100 years. Examples ranged from the earliest attempts at mating a bicycle with an engine to the space-age speed machines of today, with all the evolutionary lines of specialization in between. What began as a cheap utilitarian method of personal transport evolved, developed and became much more efficient. The exhibition demonstrated how, as time passed, the motorcycle became bigger, faster and safer as designers worked on its form to improve its function.

In the same year the Barbican Art Gallery in London presented *The Art of the Harley*, celebrating the Harley-Davidson as an icon of American culture and a vehicle for artistic expression. While the exhibition in New York dealt with the motorcycle as a mass-produced product possessing aesthetic qualities, the London show emphasized how individuals could take such an article and fashion it into a personalized statement.

The Art of the Harley exhibition celebrated the customized world of the Harley by gathering together 30 selected custom creations from around the world and presenting them like sculptures on plinths. They were shown in conjunction with taped commentaries by their respective builders alongside other exhibits such as a celebration of the customized human body with tattoos and piercings. The Hell's Angels Motorcycle Club, London, permitted a display of regalia and artefacts relating to the One Percenters, while there were examples of aftermarket

OPPOSITE
Tank Ewsichek built this Indian-fendered
FXR Harley which he calls 'Flight
DeVille'. He was also responsible for the
paintwork.

LEFT
This is the 'Purple Roadster', built by
Dave Perewitz around a softail-style
frame. It is owned by Bobby Sullivan.

ABOVE

Richard Taylor created this incredible Harman-engined bike he calls the 'Blower Bike', the main feature being the huge supercharger fitted to its right-hand side.

ABOVE RIGHT

Japanese riders often refer to Harleys as slow old tractors so, with admirable tongue-in-cheek, Didi, of Custom Ranch, Germany, created this 'John Deere' theme bike. The irony of it is that it has a high-performance S&S 1600-cc engine.

RIGHT

This softail was built by Dave Bell for his wife Jill. It is called 'Santa Fe' and features New Mexican Indian-style graphics applied by Paul Erpenbeck.

parts designed to enable the less creative to make changes to their stock Harleys.

Films and slide shows of biker rallies around the world provided a context in which the stars of the show, the customized Harley-Davidsons, could be seen, while bikes built by top American builders, together with examples from Swedish, German, French and British customizers were also included.

The exhibition was commissioned by the Barbican's curator, John Hoole, and organized by Conrad Bodman. They, with the help of many others, created a unique exhibition which attracted surprisingly little controversy in the rarefied atmosphere of the established art world, unlike the Guggenheim's *Art of the Motorcycle* exhibition, which was harshly criticized by the American intelligentsia, which considered the exhibiting of mass-produced machines inappropriate. However, this did not prevent it from being the Guggenheim's most popular show.

Moreover, the success of the exhibitions, and the fact that they were held in two of the most prestigious art galleries in the world,

has done much to change attitudes towards an art and lifestyle originating from the rebel biker.

The art of motorcycle customization seems to have begun roughly halfway through the 100-year-old history of two-wheeled transport. Specialist racing machines

existed almost from the start as motorcycle sport developed and speed improved the breed. The customization of the Harley-Davidson, as a popular movement, also grew out of the motorcyclist's natural competitiveness and thirst for ever-increasing speed. The American motorcycles of the

Florida-based Frenchman, Cyril Huze, built this custom bagger in an art-deco style. He calls it 'Miami Nice'.

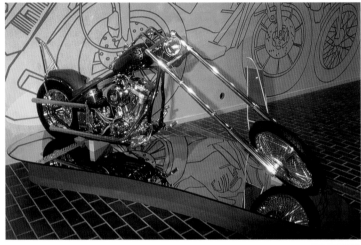

ABOVE
Nicolas Chauvin's tribute to blues legend, Stevie Ray Vaughan, graces the Barbican Art Gallery, London.

ABOVE RIGHT
'Red Viking' could only have come from one country – Sweden. Typical of the Tolle long-forked bikes, it was built by Kenth Arvidsson.

RIGHT
The exquisite Evo-engined Harley trike by Denny Franssen.

OPPOSITE
This Harley FXR was built by 'Big Steve' Morley. It was built for go as well as show as the list of modifications to the engine indicates.

forties and fifties were either Indians or Harleys. They were large machines of 750–1200cc and were built to traverse the great expanses of the American continent. These bikes had screens for protection from the weather, large steel fenders front and rear to protect the rider from dirt and spray, and large saddlebags or panniers to store tools, wet-weather gear and spare clothes. They were also equipped with lights and big comfortable seats.

Following the Second World War, the young American motorcyclist began in earnest to enjoy motorcycle sport as a leisure activity. Dirt-track racing, speedway, hill climbs and scrambles or even desert racing were popular, and production machines began to be classified, which led to Class C racing. It was not uncommon for

motorcyclists to ride to a meeting, strip their bikes down to save weight, compete, then ride home again. Thus the 'bobber' style was born.

Naturally, motorcyclists also began to imitate this chopped-down style in emulation of the racers among them, giving rise to a fashion whereby looking 'fast' was also

desirable. It was inevitable that motorcyclists, and later bikers, due to the solitary nature of the activity, should regard themselves as individuals, having a special rapport with their motorcycles and the endless road ahead. They liked to be seen as different and they liked their motorcycles to stand out from the crowd.

Riders expressed their individuality by using the basic production Harley as a starting point, changing and modifying its parts to create a style that was pleasing to the eye. As the swinging sixties progressed, so too did the practice of motorcycle customization, in parallel with the rock music, fashion, pop art and recreational drug use of these changing times. Certain individuals gained a reputation as superior bike-builders and trendsetters, and the appearance of 'lifestyle' biker magazines spread their word and their work, encouraging others to follow their lead. The art of Harley customization was at its height in the mid-sixties and some of these original creators are still at the top today.

The chopper developed once the rule book had been thrown away and the belief that form necessarily follows function was suddenly seen as no longer sacred. Apehanger bars do not function better than stock ones or even as well, but they have a form which satisfies the rider and imbues the individual with the street credibility he desires. Bikers being competitive creatures, this led to ever higher apehangers and longer front ends as a means of ensuring one did not go unnoticed

ABATE
A Brotherhood Against Totalitarian Enactments. U.S.-based riders' rights group.

Accel
Manufacturer of aftermarket ignition components.

Aermacchi
Italian motorcycle manufacturing company of which Harley-Davidson acquired a half-share in 1960 as a way to produce small-capacity lightweight motorcycles. The Japanese manufacturers dominate this sector and in 1977 Harley-Davidson sold its share back to the Italians.

AMA
The American Motorcyclist Association was the organization that coined the One Percenter label.

AMF
American Machine & Foundry, an industrial conglomerate that acquired Harley-Davison in 1969 but sold it to the management in 1980.

Apehangers
Tall handlebars so-named because the riding position requires outstretched arms.

Back Street Heroes
UK-based custom bike magazine.

Bandidos MC
A One Percenter motorcycle club founded in Texas but now worldwide.

Barger, Ralph 'Sonny'
One of the founders of the Oakland chapter of the Hell's Angels.

Bay Area
An area of San Francisco that spawned its own styles of custom Harley-Davidsons.

Beetles MC
The fictional motorcycle club led by Lee Marvin in *The Wild One*.

Big Twin
The slang term used to describe the large-capacity Harley-Davidson V-twins in order to differentiate them from the smaller-capacity Sportster models.

Billet
The term used to describe custom motorcycle parts machined from billet-aluminium on CNC milling machines.

Billy
The character played by Dennis Hopper in *Easy Rider*.

Black Rebels MC
The fictional motorcycle club led by Marlon Brando in *The Wild One*.

Blockhead
U.S. nickname for the big-twin Evolution Harley-Davidson engines.

Blower
Slang term for a supercharger.

Blue Angels MC
Longstanding and large Scottish One Percenter motorcycle club.

BMF
British Motorcycle Federation. U.K. equivalent of the AMA.

Bobber
The basic and stripped-down Indians and

Harley-Davidsons from which choppers evolved.

Buell
A sports-bike-styled motorcycle designed around a Sportster engine and now marketed by Harley-Davidson.

Bulldog Bash
Massive annual U.K. biker party run since 1987 at the drag strip outside Stratford-upon-Avon, Warwickshire, organized by HAMC England.

Chopper
A bike (often a Harley-Davidson) cut down or customized to a specific style.

Chrome Specialties Inc.
Aftermarket custom and spares component manufacturer and distributor.

Coffin tank
Once-popular custom gas tank, so-named because of its shape.

Colours
The embroidered badges of the One Percenter motorcycle clubs.

Custom Chopper Cookbook
A softback manual written by Mike Geokan that details the hard-core nuts and bolts of building custom Harleys.

Custom Chrome Inc.
Aftermarket custom and spares component manufacturer and distributor.

Davidson, Willie G.
Grandson of founder William A. Davidson, who joined Harley-Davidson's design department in 1963. He later designed the

Super Glide and XLCR models.

Daytona, Florida
Home of the annual Daytona 200, a 200-mile race around which the famous Bikeweek revolves.

Drag pipes
Drag-strip-inspired exhaust pipes.

Drag Specialties
Aftermarket custom and spares component manufacturer and distributor.

Dresser
Slang term for a standard Harley-Davidson, still fitted with the screen and panniers.

Duo Glide
Big-twin Harley-Davidson with front and rear suspension made between 1958 and 1964.

Easy Rider
The 1969 film starring Peter Fonda, Dennis Hopper and Jack Nicholson which follows a pair of bikers en route to the Mardi Gras in New Orleans on two Panhead choppers.

Easyriders
American magazine dedicated to custom Harley-Davidsons.

EL
Harley-Davidson's designation for its first overhead-valve Knucklehead of 61ci.

Electra Glide
Big-twin Harley-Davidson with front and rear suspension and electric start made from 1964 to the present.

Electra Glide in Blue
A 1973 film about a motorcycle cop.

Evo
Slang term for an Evolution-engined Harley-Davidson.

Evolution
Harley-Davidson's designation for its overhead-valve Big Twin and Sportster engines.

Fatbob
Type of bobber or early custom that featured the stock Harley-Davidson gas tank but had cut-down or removed fenders.

Fatbob tank
Slang term for the stock Harley-Davidson two-piece fuel tank. On earlier models it was the fuel and oil tank.

Fatland, Arlin
Denver, Colorado-based custom bike builder and proprietor of the famous Two-Wheelers motorcycle shop.

FEM
Federation of European Motorcyclists, a European riders' rights group.

Finks MC
Longstanding and large Australian One Percenter motorcycle club.

Fishtail pipes
Exhaust pipes so-described because they resemble a fish's tail.

FL
Harley-Davidson's designation for its first overhead-valve engines of 74ci and larger, from the Knucklehead to the Twin Cam.

Flathead
American slang for a side-valve engine, regardless of manufacturer.

Flatty (see Flathead)

Freeway
France-based custom bike magazine.

Freewheelers MC
Independent Irish One Percenter club.

Frisco-style
When the gas tank is mounted high on the frame's top tube. The fashion originated in San Francisco.

FX
Harley-Davidson's designation for its Super Glide models. The F indicates engines of 74ci and the X the use of the Sportster front end.

FXR
Harley-Davidson's designation for its rubber-mounted-engined FX models.

Garbage wagon
Derogatory slang nickname for Harley-Davidson's stock dressers.

Girder forks
A specific type of motorcycle fork that lends itself to custom bikes because of its clean lines and ease of fabrication.

HAMC
Hells Angel's. A One Percenter club founded in California and now worldwide.

Hamsters MC
An American motorcycle club dedicated to buiding and riding custom Harleys.

Hardtail
Slang term for a rigid-framed motorcycle, i.e. no rear suspension.

Harley-Davidson, Inc.
The parent company for the group of companies in business as the Harley-Davidson Motor Company, Buell Motorcycle Company and Harley-Davidson Financial Services, Inc. The Harley-Davidson Motor Company is the only major U.S.-based motorcycle manufacturer producing heavyweight motorcycles and offering a complete line of motorcycle parts, accessories, apparel and general merchandise. Buell Motorcycle Company produces sport and sport-touring motorcycles. Harley-Davidson Financial Services, Inc. provides wholesale and retail financing and insurance programmes to Harley-Davidson dealers and customers.

Harley Owners Group (HOG)
Factory-backed and -run Harley riders' organization that has worldwide members.

Hells Angel's MC (see HAMC)

High Performance
German custom-bike magazine.

Hollister, California
AMA-sanctioned races in this town became rowdy in 1947 and led to the AMA distancing itself from the so-called 1 per cent of disreputable motorcyclists.

Hydra Glide
The big-twin Harley-Davidson with hydraulic telescopic forks and rigid frames made between 1949 and 1958.

Indian
Harley-Davidson's last domestic competitor as a motorcycle manufacturer. Indians were made in Springfield, Massachusetts.

Iron Horse
Latterly *The Horse BC*, an American magazine dedicated wholly to choppers.

Knievel, Evel
Montana-born stunt motorcyclist who used Harley-Davidson XR750 motorcycles.

Knucklehead
Nickname for Harley-Davidson's first overhead-valve engine of 61ci. It is so-described because its rocker covers resemble the fingers of a clenched fist.

Laconia, New Hampshire
The venue for the huge annual bike rally based around the Loudon motorcycle race.

Liberator
European nickname for the 45-ci Harley-Davidson WLA and WLC army bikes as used by the allies in the Second World War.

The Loveless
Kathryn Bigelow's 1981 cult film, starring Willem Dafoe, about a group of riders en route to the Daytona 200 during the 1950s.

Low rider
A type of custom Harley-Davidson that rides low and close to the ground. The slang term was adopted by Harley-Davidson as a model designation.

The Lynch report
A 1965 California law enforcement agency report on One Percenter motorcycle clubs. It was widely circulated and reported though largely based on supposition.

MAG
Motorcycle Action Group. U.K.-based riders' rights pressure group.

GLOSSARY

Mask
A film based on the true story of Rocky Dennis, starring Cher and Sam Elliot, that showed a One Percenter club in a favourable light.

Milwaukee, Wisconsin
The American city where the Harley-Davidson factory is based. There is also a facility in York, Pennsylvania.

Model K
The smaller-capacity flathead Harley-Davidson introduced in 1952 that was the precursor of the Sportster.

Model V
The big-twin flathead produced by Harley-Davidson between 1930 and 1937.

Mustang tank
A popular gas tank for choppers originally sourced from the Mustang moped, though now manufactured especially for custom bikes.

NCC
Large European club established in the U.K. in 1973 and wholly dedicated to building and riding custom bikes.

Nempco
Aftermarket custom and spares component manufacturer and distributor.

Ness, Arlen
Noted and longstanding San Francisco Bay Area custom-bike builder.

Nicholson, Jack
Actor who starred with Fonda and Hopper in *Easy Rider* but also earlier in *Hell's Angels*

on Wheels, one of a series of biker exploitation movies that included *Hell's Angels '69*, *The Rebel Rousers* and *The Wild Angels*.

One Percenter
A member of a One Percenter motorcycle club.

Outlaws MC
A One Percenter club founded in Chicago and now worldwide.

Pagans MC
A One Percenter motorcycle club strong in the north-east U.S.A.

Pan
Slang for Panhead

Panhead
Overhead-valve engines made by Harley-Davidson from 1948–65. They are so-described because the rocker covers resemble upturned cooking pans.

Patch
Slang term for One Percenter colours.

Perewitz, Dave
Noted U.S. custom-bike builder from Brockton, Massachusetts

Performance Machine
Aftermarket braking component manufacturer.

P-Pad
Pillion pad rear seat.

Prism tank
Custom gas tank of a prismatic design that was popular during the seventies.

Pro-street
A recent fashion for a type of custom Harley-Davidon that takes its name from a particular drag-race class.

Quadrophenia
A 1979 British film about the mods and rockers era.

Rake and trail
The dimensions of a motorcycle's frame and forks that determine its handling characteristics.

Rat's Hole Custom Show
One of the annual attractions at Daytona Bikeweek, a custom bike show held on the boardwalk in Daytona. More recently, another has been instituted at Sturgis.

Rebels MC
Longstanding and large Australian One Percenter motorcycle club.

Rigid
A type of motorcycle frame without rear suspension made by Harley-Davidson until 1958.

Rikuo
Harley-Davidson motorcycles briefly produced under licence in Japan before the Second World War.

Risers
The brackets that clamp the handlebars to the triple trees or yokes of the forks.

RUB
A slightly derogatory acronym for the Rich Urban Bikers who became Harley-Davidson owners when it became fashionable to do so during the 1980s.

S&S
Smith & Smith, aftermarket performance custom and spares component manufacturer and distributor.

Servicar
Three-wheeled utility machine made by Harley-Davidson between 1932 and 1973 that became the basis of many custom trikes.

Shotgun pipes
A custom exhaust system where the shape of the mufflers resembles that of a pump-action shotgun.

Shovelhead
Overhead-valve engines made by Harley-Davidson from 1965–84. They are so-described because the rocker covers resemble the backs of upturned shovels. The slang term is Shovel.

Sissy bar
A rear-mounted bar that acts as a backrest for a pillion passenger but often doubles as a rear fender strut and licence-plate mount.

Smith, Donnie
A noted U.S. custom-bike builder based in Minneapolis.

Softail
A type of motorcycle frame currently manufactured by Harley-Davidson that appears rigid but has hidden rear suspension.

Solo seat
The small single seat initially fitted to Sportsters which became popular for use on choppers.

Sons of Silence MC
Longstanding and large American One Percenter motorcycle club.

Sportster
A smaller-capacity Harley-Davidson in production from 1957 to the present day. It was initially introduced to compete with imported British bikes.

Sportster tank
The graceful petrol tank from a Sportster is a popular choice for custom builders to use on other bikes.

Springer forks
An early type of sprung motorcycle fork used by Harley-Davidson until 1949 and re-introduced in the 1980s on nostalgic big twins.

Straightleg frame
The 1955–57 rigid Harley-Davidson frame sought by chopper builders because of its clean and uncluttered lines. It is known as a straightleg because its front downtubes are straight.

Stretch
The longitudinal extension of a Harley-Davidson frame in order to build a longer, lower bike.

Sturgis, South Dakota
The small town that hosts the annual Black Hills Rally founded by Pappy Hoel and the Jackpine Gypsies MC in the 1930s.

Sturgis
A limited-edition, belt-driven version of the Super Glide introduced in 1980.

Swing-arm
The pivoting rear portion of a motorcycle frame that, in conjunction with shock absorbers provides rear suspension.

Teles
Slang name for hydraulic telescopic forks.

Telescopic forks
Hydraulic telescopic forks introduced on big-twin Harley-Davidsons with the Hydra Glide of 1949.

Thunder Cycles
German-based custom bike magazine.

Twin Cam
Harley-Davidson's current air-cooled big-twin engine.

V-Rod
Harley-Davidson's liquid-cooled sports tourer.

V-twin
The term used to describe a twin-cylinder motorcycle where the cylinders are arranged in a V configuration.

V-Twin Manufacturing
Aftermarket custom, vintage and spares component manufacturer and distributor.

W&W Cycles
European aftermarket custom and spares component manufacturer and distributor.

The Wild One
A 1954 film made by Stanley Kramer, starring Marlon Brando and Lee Marvin and depicting the goings-on at Hollister in July 1947.

Wishbone frame
The 1948–55 rigid Harley-Davidson big-twin frame. It is referred to as a wishbone because of the arrangement of the front downtubes.

WL
The designation given to Harley-Davidson's 45-ci displacement V-twin motorcycles manufactured between 1937 and 1951.

WLA
WL-Army. U.S. Army-specification versions of the WL.

WLC
WL-Canada. Canadian Army-specification versions of the WL.

Wyatt
The Captain America character played by Peter Fonda in *Easy Rider*.

XA
An experimental Harley-Davidson flat-twin motorcycle based on German military BMWs and built in small numbers for the U.S. Army.

XA springers
In the post-war years, the springer forks from XA models became popular for bobbers and choppers because they were longer than those used on other Harley-Davidsons of the time.

XL
The official Harley-Davidson designation for its Sportster models.

XR
The official Harley-Davidson designation for its dirt-track-racing bikes, such as the XR750. The XR1000 was a street hot-rod version.

York, Pennsylvania
The American city where a Harley-Davidson plant is based.

Zodiac International bv
European aftermarket custom and spares component manufacturer and distributor.

Acknowledgements

The Publishers, together with John Carroll and Garry Stuart, wish to thank the following:
Arlin Fatland for his good company and cold beers; Phil Piper, of Phil's Chopper Shack, for building great choppers in Britain; Dale Richardson and Martha, in Greeley, Colorado, for their help in sourcing classic vehicles for photography; Lawayne Matthies in Dallas, Texas, for his friendship and help in Daytona and Sturgis over many years; Dale Walksler, for creating one of the world's best motorcycle museums – Wheels through Time – in Maggie Valley, North Carolina; Arlen Ness for always making his bikes available for photography; Mike Corbin for his loan of two motorcycles, which enabled the authors to ride the Pacific Coast Highway; Steve, Alan and all at Black Bear Harley-Davidson, Newmarket, England, for making bikes available for photography; Thierry Moreau, of St-Jean d'Angely, France, for supplying film, processing and aperitifs.

BIBLIOGRAPHY

MAGAZINES AND PERIODICALS

Cycle magazine
Cycle Road Test: Harley-Davidson 1200cc Super Glide
Ziff-Davis Publishing, Company November 1970

Easyriders magazine
'Wino' Willie Forkner: *All The Old Romance Retold*
Paisano Publications, September 1986

Easyriders magazine
Gary Bang: *A Junkie Hooked On Two Wheels*
Paisano Publications, March 1987

Iron Horse magazine
Look Homeward Angel
J.Q.Adams Productions Inc., December 1994

Royal Canadian Mounted Police Gazette
MacDonald, W.N.: *Outlaw Motorcycle Gangs*
Royal Canadian Mounted Police Gazette, 1994

The Horse BC magazine.
Kozik F.: *Choppers Frisco Style*
Iron Cross Ltd., September 2002

MOTORCYCLE-RELATED NON-FICTION BOOKS

Ball, K.R.
Easyriders Ultimate Customs for Harley Riders
Carlton Books Ltd., 1997

Barbican Art Gallery
The Art of the Harley
Booth-Clibborn Editions, 1998

Barger, R. Sonny
Hell's Angel. The Life and Times of Sonny Barger and the Hell's Angels Motorcycle Club
Fourth Estate, 2000

Barger, R. Sonny
Ridin' High, Livin' Free
Fourth Estate, 2002

Beerepoot, T. Grizzly
European Choppers
Uitgeverij Plukker, 1993

Davidson, W.G.
100 Years of Harley-Davidson
Bullfinch Press, AOL Time Warner Book Group, 2003

Geokan, M.
Custom Chopper Cookbook
M. Arman Publishing Inc., 1988

Guggenheim Museum
Motorcycle Mania: The Biker Book
Universe Publishing, 1998

Hanlon, D.
Riding the American Dream
Union Hill Press, 2004

Harris, M.
Bikers – Birth of a Modern-Day Outlaw
Faber and Faber, 1985

Kaye, H.R.
A Place in Hell
Holloway House Publishing Co., 1968

Lavigne, Y.
Hell's Angels
Carol Publishing Group, 1987

Lyons, D.
The Bikeriders
Twin Palms Publishers, 1997

Reid, P.C.
Well Made in America
McGraw Hill Publishing Company, 1990

Reynolds, F. and McClure, M.
Freewheelin' Frank
Grove Press Inc., 1967

Spiegel, M.
The Cycle Jumpers
Berkeley Medallion Books, 1973

Thompson, H.S.
Hell's Angels
Random House, 1966

Vermes, P.
Straightening Out The Corners
Iris Publications Inc., 1990

Wethern, G. & Colnett, V.
A Wayward Angel
Transworld Publishers Ltd., 1979

Wolf, D.R.
The Rebels: a Brotherhood of Outlaw Bikers
University of Toronto Press, 1991

Yates, B.
Outlaw Machine: Harley-Davidson and the Search for the American Soul
Little, Brown, 1999

OTHER NON-FICTION BOOKS
Downing, D. and Herman, G.
Clint Eastwood, All American Anti-Hero
Omnibus Press, 1977

Jones, J.
WWII
Leo Cooper Ltd., 1975

4. FICTION
Butler, M. and Shyrack, D.
The Gauntlet
W. H. Allen and Co., 1977

Freedman, J.F.
Against the Wind
The Penguin Group, 1991

Steinbeck, J.
The Grapes of Wrath
William Heinemann, 1939

BIBLIOGRAPHY

1. MAGAZINES AND PERIODICALS

Cycle magazine
Cycle Road Test: Harley-Davidson 1200cc Super Glide
Ziff-Davis Publishing, Company November 1970

Easyriders magazine
'Wino' Willie Forkner: *All The Old Romance Retold*
Paisano Publications, September 1986

Easyriders magazine
Gary Bang: *A Junkie Hooked On Two Wheels*
Paisano Publications, March 1987

Iron Horse magazine
Look Homeward Angel
J.Q.Adams Productions Inc., December 1994

Royal Canadian Mounted Police Gazette
MacDonald, W.N.: *Outlaw Motorcycle Gangs*
Royal Canadian Mounted Police Gazette, 1994

The Horse BC magazine.
Kozik F.: *Choppers Frisco Style*
Iron Cross Ltd., September 2002

2. MOTORCYCLE-RELATED NON-FICTION BOOKS
Ball, K.R.
Easyriders Ultimate Customs for Harley Riders
Carlton Books Ltd., 1997

Barbican Art Gallery
The Art of the Harley
Booth-Clibborn Editions, 1998

Barger, R. Sonny

Hell's Angel. The Life and Times of Sonny Barger and the Hell's Angels Motorcycle Club
Fourth Estate, 2000

Barger, R. Sonny
Ridin' High, Livin' Free
Fourth Estate, 2002

Beerepoot, T. Grizzly
European Choppers
Uitgeverij Plukker, 1993

Davidson, W.G.
100 Years of Harley-Davidson
Bullfinch Press, AOL Time Warner Book Group, 2003

Geokan, M.
Custom Chopper Cookbook
M. Arman Publishing Inc., 1988

Guggenheim Museum
Motorcycle Mania: The Biker Book
Universe Publishing, 1998

Hanlon, D.
Riding the American Dream
Union Hill Press, 2004

Harris, M.
Bikers – Birth of a Modern-Day Outlaw
Faber and Faber, 1985

Kaye, H.R.
A Place in Hell
Holloway House Publishing Co., 1968

Lavigne, Y.

Hell's Angels
Carol Publishing Group, 1987

Lyons, D.
The Bikeriders
Twin Palms Publishers, 1997

Reid, P.C.
Well Made in America
McGraw Hill Publishing Company, 1990

Reynolds, F. and McClure, M.
Freewheelin' Frank
Grove Press Inc., 1967

Spiegel, M.
The Cycle Jumpers
Berkeley Medallion Books, 1973

Thompson, H.S.
Hell's Angels
Random House, 1966

Vermes, P.
Straightening Out The Corners
Iris Publications Inc., 1990

Wethern, G. & Colnett, V.
A Wayward Angel
Transworld Publishers Ltd., 1979

Wolf, D.R.
The Rebels: a Brotherhood of Outlaw Bikers
University of Toronto Press, 1991

Yates, B.
Outlaw Machine: Harley-Davidson and the Search for the American Soul

Little, Brown, 1999

3. OTHER NON-FICTION BOOKS
Downing, D. and Herman, G.
Clint Eastwood, All American Anti-Hero
Omnibus Press, 1977

Jones, J.
WWII
Leo Cooper Ltd., 1975

4. FICTION
Butler, M. and Shyrack, D.
The Gauntlet
W. H. Allen and Co., 1977

Freedman, J.F.
Against the Wind
The Penguin Group, 1991

Steinbeck, J.
The Grapes of Wrath
William Heinemann, 1939